Hard Diplomacy and Soft Coercion

Hard Diplomacy and Soft Coercion

Russia's Influence Abroad

James Sherr

 CHATHAM HOUSE

First published in Great Britain in 2013 by
Royal Institute of International Affairs,
10 St James's Square,
London SW1Y 4LE
www.chathamhouse.org
(Charity Registration No. 208223)

Distributed worldwide by
The Brookings Institution,
1775 Massachusetts Avenue NW,
Washington DC 20036-2188, USA

British Library Cataloguing in Publication Data
A CIP catalogue record for this book is available from the British Library.

ISBN 978 1 86203 266 8

Typeset in Berling Nova by Koinonia
Printed and bound in Great Britain by Latimer Trend and Co. Ltd

The material selected for the printing of this book is Elemental Chlorine Free and
has been sourced from well-managed forests. It has been manufactured by an ISO
14001 certified mill under EMAS.

To Christopher Wenner, who taught me to be myself

Contents

Contents

About the Author

James Sherr is an Associate Fellow (and former Head) of the Russia and Eurasia Programme at Chatham House in London. He was a member of the Social Studies Faculty of Oxford University (1993–2012), a Fellow of the Conflict Studies Research Centre of the UK Ministry of Defence (1995–2008) and Director of Studies of the Royal United Services Institute (1983–85). Over many years, he has had an intensive advisory relationship with Ukraine and worked closely with a number of official and expert bodies in the West and the former Soviet region. He has published extensively on Soviet and Russian military, security and foreign policy, as well as energy security, the Black Sea region and Ukraine's effort to deal with Russia, the West and its own domestic problems.

Acknowledgments

Any book written from the heart is a work in progress. Its deficiencies emerge as soon as the ink is dry, and they mature with time. It stands to reason that any shortcomings in the pages that follow are entirely my own. The inspiration behind my ideas is not. Many, too numerous to cite here, have honed my judgement and, at times, corrected it. Others have steadied my purpose and welcomed me back from the void when my mood took me there. Some should be spared citation: long-standing friends who value their privacy and officials, serving and former, who deepened my knowledge, gave substance to my intuition and allowed themselves, when necessary, to be indiscreet in service of a higher cause.

There are others who deserve recognition and will survive it. First amongst them is James Nixey, now Head of the Russia Eurasia Programme, with whom I have worked cheek by jowl over the past four years. His energy, empathy and good humour are so legendary that they risk becoming *cliché*. The birches of the Russian *banya* are like honey compared to his editor's pen, but the text has been much improved by his hard work. One could not wish for a more honourable, resilient or capable colleague. Alex Nice, who brings intellectual tone, integrity and discernment to all of his endeavours, has left Chatham House, but not before providing significant support to the overall project and the editing of its various publications. Lubica Pollakova has earned my gratitude for providing timely and ineffably cheerful help to the project in the midst of other demanding responsibilities. I also owe a debt of gratitude to the hard work and good nature of our interns who offered tireless assistance in the tiresome job of tracking down references and making the format of the book presentable: Johannes Olschner, Rihards Kols, Katerina Tertytchnaya, Kseniya Shvedova and Annie Kennington. Nicolas Bouchet has been helpful in drawing attention to passages that required elucidation and reformulation. Margaret May, Editor of Chatham House publications, has shepherded the publication into a finished project with a watchful eye that preserves everything of value and misses nothing. She is a model for everyone who believes that editing should be an art as well as a craft.

Profound thanks are owed to John Lough, my colleague in three institutions over 25 years, for being a personally indulgent and intellectually unforgiving interlocutor. His intellectual asperity has served as foil and model in equal measure. I am equally grateful to Andrew Wood for his moral and intellectual support. His wisdom not only lingers on the palate but surfaces in these pages. Over the course of this project, Andrew Monaghan, Nicholas Redman and Craig Oliphant have done much to sustain my motivation and rescue me from error. All of them commented on parts of this manuscript with care and insight, as did Alex Pravda during an earlier stage of this project. My former CSRC colleague, Mark Smith, has also been helpful in unscrambling my thoughts and my memory for facts.

Finally, it remains for me as well as Chatham House to express gratitude to the Smith Richardson Foundation for encouraging the Russia and Eurasia Programme to undertake this project and for enabling us to do so. I am particularly grateful to Nadia Schadlow, who originally suggested that I should write on Russian soft power and then supported our decision to expand the project's remit to include Russian influence as a whole. She and her colleagues have been a pleasure to work with from conception to completion.

J.G.S.

The publication of this book marks the conclusion of a Chatham House project entitled 'The Means and Ends of Russia's Influence Abroad'. Between 2009 and 2012, three workshops were held: two on the overall theme, at Chatham House, and one on soft power, in cooperation with the Centre of Polish-Russian Dialogue and Understanding in Warsaw. The project's core contributors also published six Chatham House Briefing Papers over the course of 2011/12:

Alexander Bogomolov and Oleksandr Lytvynenko, *A Ghost in the Mirror: Russian Soft Power in Ukraine*

James Greene, *Russian Responses to NATO and EU Enlargement and Outreach*

Agnia Grigas, *Legacies, Coercion and Soft Power: Russian Influence in the Baltic States*

John Lough, *Russia's Energy Diplomacy*

James Nixey, *The Long Goodbye: Waning Russian Influence in the South Caucasus and Central Asia*

Andrew Wood, *Russia's Business Diplomacy*

1 First Principles

'The state is not pure spirit' – Leon Trotsky[1]

Definitions of influence, like definitions of aggression, are traps for the unwary. Both attempt to express in objective form something that is a matter of opinion. Like individuals, states can be unconscious of the influence they have, or they can be insufferably over-confident about it. Like individuals, states can indignantly deny that they are being influenced by others, or they can defensively blame others for their own culpabilities and failings. Definitions of power are meant to escape from these ambiguities, but they do not. Resources are tangible. Power – the utilization of resources and capacities to achieve vague or specific ends – is relational, an untidy combination of will, capacity and effects – visible and concealed, immediate and ultimate.

In his seminal work *Soft Power: The Means to Success in World Politics*, Joseph Nye defines power as 'the ability to influence the behaviour of others to get the outcomes one wants'. But he then adds that 'when we measure power in terms of the changed behaviour of others, we have first to know their preferences. ... Power always depends on the context in which the relationship exists'.[2] This truth, so frequently overlooked, is especially perilous to forget when it comes to soft power, which Nye defines as 'the ability to get what you want through attraction'.[3]

Today, there is a widespread belief that Russia has no soft power. Few, however, would claim that it has no influence. There are reasons to doubt whether soft power plays much part in it. History gives weight to

1 Leon Trotsky, *The Revolution Betrayed*, http://www.marxists.org/archive/trotsky/1936/revbet/ch11.htm.
2 Joseph S. Nye Jr, *Soft Power: The Means to Success in World Politics* (New York: PublicAffairs, 2004), p. 2.
3 Ibid., p. x.

this perception. The establishment of the Soviet Union was a sanguinary business. The greatest onslaught against it, Operation Barbarossa, was at least as sanguinary, and the apotheosis of that struggle, the Great Patriotic War, produced lessons that are easy to relearn and difficult to forget. For those who govern Russia today, the experience of the 1990s has produced hard lessons as well. It is scarcely immaterial that the USSR devoted attention to softer and more oblique forms of influence during times of weakness. Whereas Western liberals distrust any arrangement not underpinned by consent, Russian *derzhavniki* – its ideologists of 'great power' – distrust any form of consent that is not underpinned by 'hard' guarantees.[4]

For these reasons, much of Russia's present-day influence is based upon what this book calls 'soft coercion': influence that is indirectly coercive, resting on covert methods (penetration, bribery, blackmail) and on new forms of power, such as energy supply, which are difficult to define as hard or soft. As was clear from the stationing of Russian forces in the South Caucasus and Transnistria – and from the Russia–Georgia war of 2008 – military power is not an altogether spent force. In his book published thirteen years after the Soviet collapse, Nye was so unimpressed by the Russian Federation's ability to exercise soft power that he had nothing to say about it.[5]

But there is something to be said. There are four good reasons to re-examine conventional wisdom about Russia's soft power. First, the 'context in which the relationship exists' has changed at least once since the USSR collapsed in 1991. The presidency of George W. Bush not only damaged the image of the United States in much of Europe. It revived troubling questions about the universality of certain values and the right of any state or group of states to speak in their name. America's misadventures did not suddenly endow Russia with the power of attraction. But they underscored its claim to be a 'values centre' in its own right, as well as its presumptive 'right' to participate as an equal in all questions of pan-European significance. By changing the tone and much of the direction of US policy, Barack Obama has partially restored America's image in places where it had suffered. In part he

---

4 A *derzhava* is a state or power, or better still, 'state power'.
5 In a chapter on 'Others' Soft Power', he does devote attention to the Soviet Union, which 'during the Cold War' was 'America's primary competitor in soft-power resources', but says nothing about the Russian Federation (pp. 73–75ff).

has done this by bringing American actions into greater conformity with American values. But he has also defused the role that values play in foreign policy, and some observers of the 'reset' with Russia would say that he has not only defused their significance, but downgraded it.[6]

Second, even before the Eurozone crisis, the European Union had not restored Western influence to the degree that many suppose. This is not because of its proverbial disunity. Despite its divisions, the EU has been the most formidable force for integration on the European continent. It also has been at the forefront of the values debate at least as much as the United States. Its integrationist biases affect nearly every relationship it pursues and every agreement it signs. The EU makes no secret of the fact that the key to integration is harmonization of the *internal* policies of aspirant states and, with that, a transformation in the way in which institutions and economies work. These attributes have made the EU a beacon of hope for many who seek to escape from the post-communist morass. The current crisis has dimmed this beacon somewhat, but it still inspires six designated candidates for membership, three officially recognized 'potential candidates' and several other states that have declared membership their ultimate goal.

Yet there are intrinsic limits to the EU's influence. European integration is, by definition, a departure from orthodox Westphalian norms, which for over 350 years have attempted to structure international relations on the basis of respect for state sovereignty and non-intervention in internal affairs. The European project is intended to 'move beyond' these norms. It is a process of hard integration, underpinned by law and mechanisms of enforcement. Both the rigours and the purpose of this project have aroused opposition not only from Russia but from a number of established interest groups in neighbouring states. Even for many who wish to be inside the club, the toughness of EU conditionality can be cause for demoralization or resentment – especially when double standards are perceived in their application. When this conditionality is unaccompanied by membership prospects, feelings of fatalism or bitterness are that much greater. This context affords Russia scope to argue, with a degree of justice, that its own requirements for 'good-neighbourliness' – and rival integration projects, such

6 'An Open Letter to the Obama Administration from Central and Eastern Europe', *Gazeta Wyborcza*, 15 July 2009, http://wyborcza.pl/1,76842,6825987,An_Open_Letter_to_the_Obama_Administration_from_Central.html.

as the Eurasian Customs Union – are more lenient, less intrusive and more respectful of national particularities than those of the EU.

The propositions implicit in the project of a 'Europe whole and free' – that all Europeans share a common foundation of aspirations and values – have been severely tested in recent years. European enlargement and integration have promoted and produced liberty and prosperity. But even before the eurozone crisis, they were also producing their share of disruption, disorientation and discontent. Not all sections of society have benefited from the application of the *acquis communautaire,* and the power and wealth of many local elites have been threatened. EU enlargement has exposed differences in business and administrative cultures as well as national cultures. At a deeper level, it has exposed fault lines between the post-modern ethos of one Europe, 'moving beyond' nation and state, and the emphatically modern preoccupations of former Soviet states seeking to recover national consciousness and reconstitute statehood. As the issue of values has become more contentious, issues of identity have risen in importance.

The eurozone crisis has multiplied these fault lines and sharpened them. If beforehand they ran largely from east to west (and between new members and old), today they have brought to the surface significant differences of economic culture between some of the oldest members of the union. For this reason and others, the crisis has diminished the EU's moral authority among members and non-members alike, including some whose orientation is a priority interest for Russia.

The third reason to re-examine Russian soft power is given point by the second: Russia's recovery after the disruptions of the 1990s, and with it, the restoration of order, the emergence of prosperity and the revival of collective self-respect. These developments have had a demonstrable effect in Russia's neighbourhood, where some have presented 'sovereign democracy' as an example to be emulated and others as an example to be feared. The West's often enthusiastic endorsement of the changes instituted by Boris Yeltsin left bitter fruits in Russia, persuading many, not for the first time, that Western models were irrelevant or harmful to Russia's distinctive circumstances. The equation between democracy and chaos, elaborately fostered by Vladimir Putin, is not without resonance in other new, post-Soviet democracies, burdened by predatory capitalism and incompetent public authorities whose overriding preoccupation is private gain.

At the start of Putin's third *de jure* presidential term, the ills of the Russian system are also exerting their influence. But these ills are not always so visible from the vantage point of the post-Soviet 'near abroad', where conditions of life can be distinctly less favourable than they are in Russia. In countries where the Russian language still holds significant sway, the ubiquity of Russia's state-dominated media is a powerful factor skewing perceptions of Russia and the outside world. In countries where local elites lack self-confidence, Russian political figures often project purpose and resolution. Emboldened by their own political masters and endowed with resources, the representatives of Russian business can be formidable competitors and irresistible partners. In all of these spheres Russia's exponents and representatives attract as well as intimidate.

The final reason to reconsider Russian soft power is the role it plays in Russia's official policy. Although the 'coloured revolutions' of 2003–04 in Georgia and Ukraine were a catalytic moment, Russia had already invested considerable 'humanitarian' resources in what its June 2000 *Concept of Foreign Policy* called the 'formation of a good-neighbourly belt along the perimeter of Russia's borders'. In recent years, the geographical scope of this activity has widened, and in the former Soviet Union its intensity has deepened. Today the instruments of soft power include public relations and public diplomacy, print and broadcast media, the Russian Orthodox Church, commissions to correct 'distortions' of history, and a raft of state-supported foundations designed to unite 'compatriots', propagate the Russian language and expand an appreciation of Russian culture abroad.

A broader purpose of this study is to examine how Russian approaches to power and influence have evolved and how they differ from those of their Western counterparts. Chapter 2 sets out the historical and institutional factors that condition present-day Russian methods of advancing the country's political and economic interests, as well as group or sectoral interests that might not always serve those of the state. These interests have changed, and they are changeable. Just as much as the United Kingdom, Russia bears witness to the proposition that history is the product of human will and decision. But it also confirms the wisdom of Joseph de Maistre's axiom: 'we do not invent ourselves'. In the USSR, ideological saturation bred ideological cynicism. Yet the ideological overtones of Western policy in the 1990s (which Konstantin Kosachev, Head of the Federal Agency for CIS Countries and International Humanitarian Cooperation, has termed 'Western messianism'[7]) caused umbrage in Russia, something that the stridency of the Bush years only increased. This fresh and recent experience has also revived respect for continuities with the Soviet past and with pre-Soviet national and state traditions and symbols. The past twenty years are a reminder that it is easier to abandon ideologies than the habits of mind they produce. The fact that we refashion our history to suit our needs only shows that history matters.

Chapter 3 relates this discussion to the ends that Russian influence is designed to serve in the former USSR and a diminished but unmistakably extant Euro-Atlantic community. Many of these aims are conflicted. From the outset, Vladimir Putin expressed the hope that 'all those who want to cooperate with Russia could feel comfortable'.[8] But Russian policy habitually undermines this sense of comfort by 'making use of weakness' and 'strengthening the coercive component' of relations with neighbouring states, and by requiring others to alter their practices in order to accommodate Russia's interests.[9] Like their predecessors, Putin and Dmitry Medvedev maintain that Russia is part of Europe. But they also maintain that Russia is too exceptional, in the words of Yeltsin's former spokesman, to 'simply dissolve into the *schéma* of European diplomacy'.[10] Under the mantle of the slogan that 'there can be no security in Europe without Russia', Russia insists that its relations with the North Atlantic Treaty Organization (NATO) and the EU develop on the basis of 'equality'. But it is not content to remain an equal external party. It seeks institutional changes, a right to shape rules and, especially with regard to NATO, *de jure* authority over relations with other external parties, particularly those that lie within its presumptive 'sphere of privileged interests'. Without accepting the obligations, constraints and risks, let alone values, that entitle NATO and EU members to assert equal rights with respect to one another,

---

7 Konstantin Kosachev, 'Russia and the West: Where the Differences Lie', *Russia in Global Affairs*, No. 4, October–December 2007.

8 Vladimir Putin, 'Russia at the Turn of the Millennium', December 1999, cited in Richard Sakwa, *Russia's Choice* (Routledge, 2nd edn 2008), p. 52.

9 Oleksandr Potekhin, 'Russian Foreign Policy Trends under President Putin', *Monitoring* (Kyiv: Centre for Peace, Conversion and Foreign Policy of Ukraine), 30 May 2000.

10 Vyacheslav Kostikov, *Trud [Labour]*, 22 February 1994.

it also claims a right to participate in their deliberations.[11] In equally 'principled' terms, Russia opposes a 'return to the Cold War', but it also seeks material revisions to the settlement that concluded it.

This stance reflects a number of factors: historical and geopolitical asymmetries, ambivalence, apprehension, manipulation and ambition. In all respects, changing *how* others think about Russia and its role in the world is at least as important to Russian policy-makers as changing *what* they think about the specific issues bedevilling relations: terms of investment and trade, energy security, compliance with treaties and agreements, policy in the 'common neighbourhood', visa regimes, border protection and observance of European standards (and OSCE commitments) regarding human rights. The desire of Western countries to remove obstacles and create trust runs headlong into the view that little of substance will be achieved until a 'reformatting' of relations takes place.[12]

The subject of Chapter 4 is the currency of influence that Russia has developed, much of it distinctive to it and unsettling to others. This part of the study examines three sources of influence – business, energy and culture – and the methods used to turn them into instruments of policy. It brings two issues into focus. First, even culture, seen as a primary source of soft power by Nye, can be promoted by hard methods. Does that make cultural diplomacy soft or hard? Second, positive influence does not necessarily advance policy. Microsoft, Apple and Facebook exemplify American virtues of openness, ingenuity and opportunity. Yet they produced no political dividends for George W. Bush at all. The 2012 Olympics and Paralympics portrayed Britain as a country comfortable with tradition, heterodoxy and, above all, itself. But they are unlikely to change perceptions of the war in Afghanistan or help Prime Minister David Cameron in his negotiations with

---

11 As affirmed by Konstantin Kosachev, Chairman of the State Duma Committee on International Affairs, '"[e]qual" participation implies Russia's full-fledged admission to the "Euro-Atlantic Club" and its real influence on the decision-making process'. But unlike Russia's foreign minister, he asserts that this requires Russia to 'join, not just in word but in action, the common system of democratic values and decisions'. Konstantin Kosachev, 'Three Birds with One Stone?', *Russia in Global Affairs*, November 2010, http://eng.globalaffairs.ru/number/Three-Birds-with-One-Stone-15146.

12 In Kosachev's words, 'Europe is absolutely not motivated to reform itself. Russia, which feels uncomfortable in the current situation, unlike Germany, the US, Switzerland or China, is seeking to reformat the collective security system'. Ibid.

the eurozone. In the same vein, the influence of the Russian language in the former Soviet Union does not necessarily enhance trust of the Russian state. Influence is only a political tool when it induces the recipient to act in a desired manner. It is most unlikely to do so if the recipient's character and preferences are not understood.

Chapter 5 attempts to arrive at a strategic audit. Have Russia's methods of influence advanced its aims? Is Russia's soft power perceived as soft by those who experience it? By adopting three levels of analysis – the strategic, the operational and the tactical – it will be possible to advance some conclusions as to where Russian influence is effective, where it is counterproductive and why.

The study puts its emphasis on divergences between Russian and Western thinking, not because Russia is *sui generis*, but because it is the West's differences with Russia that define its difficulties with it. Many of these differences are rooted in the system of power. In Yeltsin's time an independent kleptocracy threatened to privatize the state. Today a state kleptocracy distributes rent, profit and property as it sees fit. The progressive fusion of money and power in Russia, the emergence of bespoke jurisprudence and the migration of connoisseurs of hard power into corporate boardrooms have implications that not all Western businesses or politicians grasp. In its Darwinian form, Western business seeks to destroy competitors. In Russia it is equally normal for businesses to destroy partners or devour them, and not every Western participant in a joint venture is prepared for this. The absence of clear borders between state and private, political and economic, lawful and criminal are endemic to what Vadim Kononenko and Arkady Moshes call a 'network state'.[13] As Vladislav Inozemtsev has written, 'Russia has built a system in which the execution of state powers has become a monopolistic business .... Political problems are solved as if they were commercial ones, and commercial ones as if they were political.'[14]

This study takes issue with the view that Russian practice in politics and business is not appreciably different from what it is 'anywhere else'. If its subject were China, Saudi Arabia or India, it would do the same. The interplay of tradition and experience in Russia has not only

13 Vadim Kononenko and Arkady Moshes, *Russia as a Network State: What Works in Russia When State Institutions Do Not* (London: Palgrave Macmillan, 2011).

14 Vladislav Inozemtsev, 'Neo-Feudalism Explained', February 2011, http://postindustrial.net/2011/02/neo-feudalism-explained/.

produced ironic questions such as 'against whom are you waging friend-ship?', but a *modus operandi* that earns the respect of enemies, seduces strangers and alienates friends.[15] It also produces a morally uncompli-cated approach to power and its uses, an obliviousness to contradic-tion and a willingness to bully others and disregard the rules that they respect – a 'cynical and pragmatic' policy that throws risk-averse elites in Western democracies off balance and achieves what neither hard power nor soft power could accomplish on its own.[16] Asymmetries in methods and discourse multiply problems caused by differences of interest, which also exist and should not be underestimated.

The final purpose of the study, addressed in Chapter 6, is to ask where Western policy might be in need of adjustment. It is axiomatic that the West has bigger issues to contend with than Russia. But the axiom is of dubious relevance. In areas ranging from Afghanistan, Iran and Syria to the future of the Arctic – not to say any issue requiring sanction by the UN Security Council – Russia is an important variable in the art of the possible, and it knows how to remind the West of this. In other areas, such as the future of nuclear weapons and the non-proliferation regime, energy security, the South Caucasus, the Caspian and the 'common European neighbourhood', it is a critical player, the key to many solutions and the source of many problems. The axiom is also spurious. Russia does not 'compete' with the West's primary security threats. It is not always a partner, but it is not an enemy. Unlike the Taliban, Iran, North Korea or Al-Qaeda, a more advantageous policy towards Russia does not require boots on the ground, investment in infrastructure security or elaborate missile defences (Russian paranoia notwithstanding). What it does require are measures that are intellectually and institutionally demanding and, quite often, politically difficult.

15 My paraphrase of the neat Russian play on words, *protiv kogo viy druzhite*, as the literal translation – 'against whom are you befriending?' is both clumsy and obscure.
16 Even among moderate and respected political thinkers, such as Sergey Karaganov, these differences are often a source of pride – e.g., 'Russia firmly and consistently revised the rules of the game that had been imposed on it in the years of its revolu-tionary collapse. The revision culminated in Putin's Munich speech in 2007 and in Medvedev's tough response in August 2008. But even before that, Russian diplomacy ceased to be revisionist and became cynical and pragmatic. And it remains so to this day'. Sergey Karaganov, 'Lucky Russia', *Russia in Global Affairs*, March 2011, http://eng.globalaffairs.ru/pubcol/Lucky-Russia-15154.

Policy towards Russia also requires a strategic approach. This is not because 'Russians think strategically', though they sometimes do. More frequently, in operational terms, Russian leaders have shown that they know what they want and know how to get it (e.g. in the South Caucasus in summer 2008). Yet just as often, in both the Soviet period (e.g. the 1979 invasion of Afghanistan) and recent times (e.g. the 2007 riots in Tallinn), they have behaved with ruthless or reckless opportunism. And on more occasions than one, they have displayed indirection, introversion and confusion. A strategic approach is required for three reasons. First, when the Russian state defines its goal and its opponent, it acts with unnerving concentration and intensity. Second, Russia tends to combine means and methods that Western minds prefer to differentiate and Western bureaucracies compartmentalize. And third, it is required as an antidote to the addiction to 'process', the faith that common institutions will harmonize conflicting interests and the inclination of a number of decision-makers to confuse principles with policy.

Redefining the definitions

As Joseph Nye acknowledges, the relationship between hard and soft power is imperfect.[17] Where Russia is concerned, this is an understatement. This is less because 'the types of behaviour between command and co-option range along a spectrum' than because of the tendency of Russian actors to combine hard and soft approaches in particular practices and as a general *modus operandi*. The expression *prinudit' k druzhbe* – 'coerce into friendship' – gives flavour to this queasy reality. Sir Isaiah Berlin had a historical explanation for this: Russia's pre-Enlightenment conviction that 'man is one, not many'.[18]

For this reason it is easier, and possibly fairer to the subject, to discuss Russian approaches to influence in the round rather than any specific form of power. But without intellectual precision, it will not be possible to expose shortcomings in definitions of 'power', 'hard power', 'influence' and 'soft power' that are deceptively precise and unfair to

17 Nye, *Soft Power*, p. 7.
18 Sir Isaiah Berlin lecture on Russia and the Enlightenment (January 1975) in the lecture series on the Eighteenth-century Enlightenment, held under his chairmanship at Wolfson College, Oxford.

the subject. A study of the Russian understanding of these concepts needs to avoid two pitfalls: definitions that are purely Russo-centric (and inadvertently self-justifying) and definitions built on cultural assumptions that obscure what is distinctive about Russian thinking and practice. If definitions are to meet the 'Russia test', they must be able to examine Russian practice without losing the ability to assess and question it.

The merit of Nye's definition of power as 'the ability to influence the behaviour of others to get the outcomes one wants' is that it is relational. As he points out, a second and more old-fashioned definition, 'the possession of capabilities or resources that can influence outcomes', is not.[19] Nye's definition is also enlightened, because it is predicated on achieving a positive end. But the Russian conception of power, and even more the exercise of it, often fails to meet this test. In the Russian convention, power can just as readily apply to the ability to dominate or damage others or to 'neutralize' opponents, whether or not any positive end is served by doing so. The unexpressed assumption is that these accomplishments have value in themselves.

What is even more noteworthy about the Russian and Soviet tradition is the paucity of discussion about power as such. In the USSR, such questions were almost exclusively the preserve of military scientists, and their work measured and catalogued, to tedious and exhaustive degree, the geographical, material, social and 'moral' factors of national 'power'. Analysis of power in relational terms was subordinated to discussion of the wider relationship between war, revolution and politics, and the Soviet Union generated a corpus of 'military-theoretical' writing on the subject. Paradoxically, the Soviet conception that comes closest to Nye's is that of Lenin who, as a student of Clausewitz, was at pains to remind his interlocutors that war is 'a tool of policy'. As noted in Chapter 2, Lenin and his followers were also determined to bring out the 'class-based', i.e. horizontal and transnational, dimension of these issues.

Despite the Gorbachevian interlude, the most influential post-Soviet addition to this corpus of thought was not provided by 'new thinkers', but by old ones. The revival of the late nineteenth- and early twentieth-century discipline of geopolitics, its reorientation to the 'global market' and the 'intensification of struggle to expand the limits' of influence

19 Nye, *Soft Power*, p. 3.

in a 'divided world' was given impetus and direction by a number of Russian academics, notably K. S. Gadzhiev, who produced the leading Russian university textbook on the subject in 1994.[20] The revival of the view of states as sovereign 'spatial-geographical phenomena' engaged in a struggle to dominate 'space' can be seen *inter alia* in recent Russian military doctrines, which define as 'dangers' and 'threats' the 'presence' (rather than the purpose) of foreign armed forces in areas adjacent to Russia. Russian geopolitics is austere and adamantine realism perfected in an intellectual space in which the voices of liberal thinkers are muffled – or heard more audibly outside Russia than within it.

These foundations provide a good platform for understanding why the exercise of Russian power has often defeated its goals. Rather than internalizing Russian views, power is simply defined here as *the utilization of resources and capacities to achieve one's ends with respect to others.* Hard power is defined as *the ability to compel others to comply with our wishes by means of force or other direct forms of coercion.*

Influence, the core focus of this study, is less difficult to define in a Russian context than one might suppose. In part, this is because influence played a strong part in the Leninist tradition. It was also at the heart of Mikhail Gorbachev's 'new thinking', and for good or ill, in its more covert and incisive forms it has been a core function of Soviet and Russian intelligence services since the formation of the *Cheka* in 1917. In this study, influence is defined as *the ability to persuade or induce others to respect or defer to one's wishes without resort to force or explicit threats. How* this is done brings out some significant differences between Russian and Western practice. But the definition is equally applicable to both.

This study also treats diplomacy as a form of influence. Many definitions of diplomacy evoke Nye's criticism of definitions of power: they are static, rather than relational. The Oxford English Dictionary defines it as 'the profession, activity or skill of managing international relations', as if it were a form of administration.[21] Harold Nicolson suggests that more is involved when he describes it as 'an ordered conduct of relations between one group of human beings and another

20 K. S. Gadzhiev, *Vvedenie v geopolitiku* [*Introduction to Geopolitics*] (Moscow: Logos, 1994, revised edn 1998), p. 9 and *passim.*
21 Similarly, G.R. Berridge defines it as: 'official channels of communication employed by members of a system of states'. *Diplomacy Theory from Machiavelli to Kissinger* (London: Palgrave Macmillan, 2001).

group alien to themselves'.[22] In this study diplomacy is defined as *the art of presenting one's own policy in a way calculated to influence the policy of others*. As practised in Russia and many other countries, the techniques of diplomacy can include informing, persuading, warning, dissembling and lying.

It is the notion of soft power that presents the greatest challenges. The concept is easier to define than understand. Nye's definition – 'the ability to get what you want through attraction' – gets to the heart of the matter. But his elaboration of the concept invites scrutiny. 'Soft power', he tells us, 'is a staple of daily democratic politics'.[23] In three respects, he skews the equation in favour of liberal democracies.

First, he wrote in 2004 that 'The countries that are likely to be more attractive and gain soft power [are those] whose dominant culture and ideas are closer to prevailing global norms (which now emphasize liberalism, pluralism and autonomy).'[24] Today Nye's proposition appears nostalgic. When Lavrov said that the West was 'losing its monopoly of the globalization process',[25] he was not mistaken, and the financial crisis had not even begun.

Second, Nye stated that 'When a country's culture includes universal values and its policies promote values and interests that others share, it increases the probability of obtaining its desired outcomes. ... Narrow values and parochial cultures are less likely to produce soft power.'[26] But part of Russia's appeal in countries distrustful of the United States is that it has opposed 'universal values' and yet improved the lives of its citizens. The fact that it is a 'sovereign democracy' *not* seeking imitation makes it more comfortable to deal with for many. Where Russia has made a point of appealing to 'civilizational ties' and a 'common history'– notably the Slavic parts of the former USSR – it has often aroused resentment.

Third, the emphasis on values is itself a Western bias. Russia has not pitched its appeal to values but to identities. Identity politics is not

---

22 Harold Nicolson, *Diplomacy* (London: Oxford University Press, 1963). He adds that it stems from 'the need to be informed of the ambitions, weaknesses and resources of those with whom one hopes to deal', pp. 17, 26.

23 Nye, *Soft Power*, p. 6.

24 Ibid., pp. 31–32.

25 Sergei Lavrov, 'The Present and the Future of Global Politics', *Russia in Global Affairs*, No. 2, April–June 2007, http://eng.globalaffairs.ru/number/n_8554.

26 Nye, *Soft Power*, p. 11.

the same as values politics, and because identity is based on affinity more than attraction, its hold is often deeper. Some in the 'near abroad' who dislike much of what they see in Russia nevertheless feel culturally connected to it and relate to its way of life; while impressed with standards of living in the EU, they find ways of life there unfamiliar and even alien to their own norms and experience.

In two other respects, Nye raises more questions than he answers. First, power of attraction over whom? Although Nye states that 'soft power does not belong to the government in the same way that hard power does', his view is remarkably state-centric. The post-Soviet world is a fragmented one composed not only of states, but of diverse communities, sectoral interests and transnational ties – and, as in other parts of the world, inequalities of wealth and power. Without a grasp of what Lenin called the 'who-whom' and the 'correlation of forces' within states, and what Lavrov has on a number of occasions called 'network diplomacy', it will not be possible to assess Russia's ability to attract.

Second, Nye asserts that soft power is power through attraction 'rather than coercion or payments'.[27] But what is meant by 'payments'? The prosperity of the United States, central to its soft power, would not exist without payments. Does Nye mean *improper* payments? By whose standard should propriety be judged? If the pervasiveness of rent-seeking intermediaries in post-Soviet business is improper, is the prominence of other rent-seeking intermediaries in Western business (e.g. lawyers, auditors and consultants) proper? How should payments –corruption – be treated when they are not discrete events but part of an economic culture? Inozemtsev's observation is to the point: 'What Westerners would call corruption is not a scourge of the system but the basic principle of its normal functioning.'[28] That 'system' is also a business model centred on networks rather than markets, patronage rather than competition, protection rather than openness and 'understandings' rather than rules. For many 'groups of influence' in the former USSR and Central Europe, that model is attractive, not to say contagious, and the rules-based Western model constraining. Should the post-communist business model be excluded from the discussion of soft power because it is 'corrupt' or included because it is attractive?

27 Ibid., p. x.
28 Inozemtsev, 'Neo-Feudalism Explained'.

The question does not admit of a dogmatic answer.

The definition of soft power employed in this work is thus more specific but also more open-ended than Nye's: *the ability to influence the preferences and behaviour of others through affinity or attraction.*

Limits and ambitions of the study

This book is about less and more than its title suggests. Its subtitle, 'Russia's Influence Abroad', raises the question, 'Who in Russia is seeking to influence whom?' Yet what follows is a study neither of elites nor of decision-making. These are difficult subjects in themselves that need to be approached with caution. Russia's mode of decision-making, like its mode of governance, is not only opaque, but hierarchical, person-alized and often arbitrary. On specific questions of importance, the institutions one would expect to find at the centre of things, such as the Ministry of Foreign Affairs, might not even be consulted. The replacement of the Yeltsin-era 'multi-voicedness' with Putin's *'vertikal'* has not simplified but complicated the picture. The role of money and financial interest complicates it further. Decisions there are, but one will look in vain for a decision-making process. This is not the place to do justice to these issues.

In these pages the term 'Russia' is defined by its context. It means the people who hold power in Russia or the people who decide the matter in question. An effort is made to be more specific where this is both necessary and possible. In adopting these conventions, the intent is not to imply that Russia is a 'unitary rational actor' – a stance certain to earn a *fatwa* from the academic world. The United States is not a unitary rational actor, but that does not make 'US policy' an impermissible term. In any state, it is important to understand where disputes begin and end. The Russian military and security establishments are rent with discord over prerogatives, priorities and resources, but that does not mean that they are at odds over NATO enlargement, US global policy or missile defence. Today, Russian liberals and dissenters are united in their opposition to Vladimir Putin, but that does not mean they all opposed the war with Georgia or take issue with the view that Ukraine is an 'artificial state'. When it comes to the issues under consideration in this study, there is more consensus than in many other areas that students of Russia write about.

A second limitation is that this book is unabashedly Western-centric. For that reason alone, some will regard it as dated even before it is read. For many it is axiomatic that 'the post Cold-War world is being replaced by a post-Western world in which China and Russia are playing an increasingly important role'.[29] It is not difficult to chart the growing visibility of Sinophiles, pragmatic and ideological, in Russian policy discourse. A common commitment to state sovereignty, multipolarity, opposition to American hegemony, trade and military ties, and regional security cooperation define a mutually important relationship.

But the Russia–China relationship is not yet of strategic, let alone global significance, and it is questionable whether it will assume this significance any time soon. Russians are far from being of one mind about this relationship's prospects and implications. In 2011 the influential Council on Foreign and Defence Policy asserted that 'China's growing might is pushing Russia closer to Europe and the United States' and spoke despairingly of the dynamics of 'Finlandization' in the relationship.[30] What is more, the ambitions of Russia's Sinophiles are not shared in China, which looks at Russia through a judiciously pragmatic prism and, for all its opposition to US hegemony, considers its relationship with the United States to be of far greater importance.

More significantly, Russia's own historical experience, its superpower mindset and its desire to be a 'swing power' between Asia and the West create cognitive and cultural obstacles to the type of relationship that the more ambitious Sinophiles seek. As Bobo Lo has observed, 'Russian foreign policy arises out of an indigenous imperial tradition, a European cultural-historical heritage, and an America-centric geopolitical culture. The West continues to supply the principal external reference points, even if many of these are perceived negatively.'[31] These ingredients do not argue for the kind of breakthrough that would alter the central place that the United States and Europe have in Russian interests.

A third caveat is that this book is neither a comparative nor an

29 Andrey Tsygankov, *What is China to Us? Westernizers and Sinophiles in Russian Foreign Policy*, Russie.Nei.Visions, No. 45 (Paris: IFRI, December 2009), p. 5.

30 Council on Defence and Foreign Policy, *Russia Should Not Miss Its Chance*, Analytical Report, (Moscow: Valdai Discussion Club), November 2011, pp. 28, 30.

31 Bobo Lo, *Axis of Convenience: Moscow, Beijing and the New Geopolitics* (Washington, DC: Brookings/Chatham House, 2008), p. 4.

empirical study. Readers will look in vain for an assessment of how Russian influence in Georgia compares with that in Ukraine or whether its influence in Moldova has risen or fallen since Putin came to power. They will be even more disappointed if they expect to find a methodology, a research design or a theoretical critique. The study aims to advance understanding of Russian thinking, not IR theory. It falls within the domain of what we used to call the humanities rather than what we now call social science.

The purpose here is to analyse Russia's approach towards influencing others. It tries to explain why this approach has emerged, how it has evolved and how it affects Russia's environment and that of the West. Yet the assessment covers Russian foreign policy as well as its methods. The latter cannot be divorced from the objectives they are meant to serve.

Russia's views of influence form an important part of what Witold Rodkiewicz has called its foreign policy culture.[32] Extrapolating from Jack Snyder's definition of strategic culture, Rodkiewicz defines this as 'the sum total of ideas, conditioned emotional responses and patterns of habitual behaviour that members of the national foreign policy community have acquired through instruction or imitation or share with each other'.[33]

As Stephen Blank has said, such ideas 'do not originate in the stratosphere and then descend to earth'.[34] They emerge in response to particular conditions, a historical experience and the lessons drawn from it. Russia's current leaders have made it clear that they regard this historical experience as a source of legitimacy and inspiration for the state.

Consistent with this framework, three propositions are advanced. First, today's Russian state has inherited a culture of influence deriving from the Soviet and Tsarist past. It bears the imprint of doctrines, disciplines and habits acquired over a considerable period of time in

32 'Gruzja w kontekście rosyjskich koncepcji polityki zagranicznej po 1991 r' ['Georgia in the Context of Russian in the Context Russian Foreign Policy Conceptions after 1991'], paper presented at the 7th St Grigol Peradze Annual Caucasian Conference, University of Warsaw, 5 December 2008.

33 Jack Snyder, *The Soviet Strategic Culture: Implications for Limited Nuclear Operations* (Santa Monica, CA: Rand Corporation, 1977), p. 8.

34 Stephen J. Blank, 'The Sacred Monster: Russia as a Foreign Policy Actor', in Stephen J. Blank (ed.), *Perspectives on Russian Foreign Policy* (Carlisle, PA: Strategic Studies Institute, US Army War College, 2012), p. 97.

relations with subjects, clients and independent states. The problems that bedevil present-day relations between the West and Russia are not simply the product of 'Cold War mindsets'. Second, the internal factor is central to an understanding of the international one and state-centric, 'black box' approaches distort far more than they reveal about how Russia behaves and why. Third, Russia is not better at conducting foreign policy than other leading states, but it has a metabolism and methodology of its own. Ignorance of the precedents, fears and ambitions that inform this policy will produce a recipe for misjudgment in the West and unpleasant surprises for it. A formulaic approach to resolving differences will only repackage them, and a 'rational actor' schematic of Russia's 'needs' will produce frustration.

2 The Pedigree of Ideas

'All Russian history produces a transitional society, which never succeeds in acquiring a final, stable form.' – Vladimir Pastukhov[1]

Less than two years after the Bolshevik revolution, Lenin wrote that 'there is no more erroneous or more harmful idea than the separation of foreign from internal policy'.[2] This dictum has all the solemnity of a platitudinous truth. Were there no connection between the internal constitution of states and their external policy, this study would be entirely misconceived. But Lenin's quotation is both less and more revealing than it appears to be at first sight.

The Westphalian 'society of states' established in 1648 and still largely extant makes it difficult for any country to pursue foreign policy as if it were an extension of policy at home. To this day, the sovereignty of states and the principle of non-intervention remain – with qualified and contentious exceptions – grounded in international law and the United Nations Charter. Where states are internally cohesive and able to defend themselves, their status is underpinned by power as well as law. But where they lack internal cohesion and legitimacy, international and domestic politics are difficult to keep apart. It is precisely this reality that Lenin had in mind.

He was not the first to consider how the interstate system and a transnational ideology could be reconciled in theory and practice. Following the Congress of Vienna in 1815, Austria's Chancellor, Klemens von Metternich, drew a distinction between the territorial and social dimensions of international affairs very similar to the dual

---

1 Vladimir Pastukhov, *Restavratsiya vmesto reformatsii* [*Restoration Instead of Reform*] (Moscow: OGI, 2012), p. 104.
2 *'Vneshnyaya politika russkoy revoliutsii'* [The External Policy of the Russian Revolution], in *Sochinenie* [Collected Works] (Moscow: State Publishing House of Political Literature, Institute of Marx-Engels-Lenin, 1949), p. 67.

foreign policy (state and class) that Lenin articulated after 1920: a policy that remained the *modus operandi* of the Soviet regime until the mid-Gorbachev era.[3] Between 1815 and the Crimean War, the Holy Alliance between Austria, Prussia and Russia promulgated, in conservative and 'legitimist' form, a doctrine of intervention foreshadowing the Brezhnev doctrine more than a century later.[4] From the mid-nineteenth century, liberalism also became a factor in international politics. When British Prime Minister Lord Palmerston supported Italy but not Poland in its quest for statehood, he illustrated the tension between principle and Realpolitik that still exists today.

The end of the Cold War has brought an intensely ideological century to a close. But the notion that 'realism' can now keep values behind state frontiers is profoundly unhistorical. The Westphalian system disciplined the relationship between internal and external affairs, but never severed it. The growth of the 'national principle' in nineteenth-century Europe tested these disciplines to the limit, and in 1914 they collapsed. In the twenty-first century, a host of new factors knit domestic and foreign affairs together. The mobility of capital and ideas has diminished the force of sovereignty. International organizations and 'regimes', from the International Monetary Fund and the World Trade Organization to the Organization for Security and Cooperation in Europe (OSCE), legitimize the scrutiny of internal affairs, even if they only do so in specific domains and with a government's formal consent. As noted in Chapter 1, the values of the EU are not merely the peculiarities of member states, but a political force in Europe. Paradoxically, NATO has become even more of a values-based organization after the Cold War than it was at its height.[5] Twenty years after the end

3 'They [international relations] have a political side, and they have a second that I cannot designate otherwise than with the qualifier *revolutionary*'. Klemens von Metternich, *Mémoires*, v. 5, p. 373, cited in Carsten Holbraad, *The Concert of Europe: A Study in German and British International Theory, 1815–1914* (London: Longman, 1970).

4 On this basis, Russia assisted Austria in crushing the Hungarian revolution of 1849. Even after the Crimean War and tensions in the Balkans damaged this solidarity, it briefly resurfaced in the 1872–73 League of Three Emperors. M.S. Anderson, *The Eastern Question 1774-1923: A Study in International Relations* (London: Macmillan, 1966), pp. 179ff.

5 During the Cold War, NATO was an 'alliance of democracies' with non-democratic exceptions: Portugal (a founding member) under António Salazar (1949–68), Greece under the regime of the Colonels (1967–74) and Turkey under three periods of military intervention (1960–61, 1971 and 1980–83). No such state would be able to join NATO today.

of the Cold War, there remains a connection between value systems, the type of place Europeans wish to live in and geopolitics.

The imperial inheritance

Lenin's maxim was pertinent in Russia well before he was born, and it retains this pertinence some ninety years after his death. Tsarist Russia was an autocracy and a patrimonial state. At the beginning of the twentieth century, its legal and institutional character distinguished it from every other great power in Europe. The imperial authority was constrained neither by countervailing institutions nor by law. Even among the landed aristocracy, property rights, exercised *de facto*, were enjoyed in theory by the Tsar alone. Alexander II's impressive efforts to introduce a European legal structure were truncated by his assassination. Only the nascent liberal movement showed an understanding of the legal culture that had shaped modern Europe. The country's Slavophiles and radicals despised European legal traditions in equal measure, and the latter regarded personal liberty in only instrumental or, in the case of the Bolsheviks, cynical terms. As Leonard Schapiro observed:

> In Russia the whole fabric of liberty still remained to be constructed at the turn of the eighteenth century. ... Even by the second half of the nineteenth century the process of safeguarding civil rights which had virtually been completed all over Western Europe had barely begun. Of political liberty, there was no trace.[6]

Russia was also a multinational empire. Unlike Britain and France – states that acquired empires – the Russian state and empire were coterminous and all but indistinguishable. This fact was not only an existential concern, but an enduring stimulant to what John LeDonne has called a 'grand strategy' to dominate the Baltic, the Black Sea and the Caspian.[7] Throughout the eighteenth century until the rise of Napoleon, and indeed for at least a decade following his defeat, this strategy was in the ascendant, and until the Industrial Revolution, it

6 Leonard Schapiro, 'Liberalism in Russia', *Times Literary Supplement*, 10 January 1958, republished in the collection of Schapiro's essays: Ellen Dahrendorf (ed.), *Russian Studies* (London: Collins Harvill, 1986), p. 47.

7 John LeDonne, *The Grand Strategy of the Russian Empire, 1650–1831* (Oxford University Press, 2004), p. 217.

was underpinned by economic as well as military power. Much of its *modus operandi* – the creation of client societies and states, the incorporation of client elites into the empire's governing establishment, the use of security guarantees to foster subjugation, reliance on intimidation and 'awesomeness', and a calculated ambiguity about what was domestic and what was foreign[8] – survives to the present day.

The Russian Federation and its post-Soviet neighbours remain burdened by this heritage of autocracy and empire. The Bolshevik Revolution and civil war not only arrested but extirpated the countervailing civic and constitutional tendencies that had emerged during Alexander II's reign and recovered momentum after 1905. Five legacies of the Tsarist inheritance warrant mention here.

The first is a problematic correspondence between national and state borders. Until 1939–40, none of the western Ukrainian territories were ever governed by Moscow. Ukrainians in the Russian empire were coterminous with Ukrainians residing in the Austro-Hungarian province of Galicia and, after 1920, Poland. Today, an estimated three million Ukrainians reside in the Russian Federation. Before 1772, the territory now known as Belarus lay almost entirely within the Polish–Lithuanian Commonwealth and, under the 1921 Treaty of Riga, its westernmost territories were assigned to the newly reconstituted Polish state. Long after the Russo-Persian and Russo-Turkish wars (1826–29) that gave Persian Armenia and Eastern Armenia to Russia, the majority of Armenians continued to reside in the Ottoman empire. Azeris, Uzbeks and Tajiks incorporated into the Russian empire also lived in other jurisdictions, and today many continue to reside outside their titular states.

The Russian population was and remains a special case. From 1889 (and particularly after 1904), Russian migration to non-Russian parts of the empire was officially encouraged for a combination of economic, political and security reasons.[9] The policy was a foreshadowing of

8 Thus the notional jurisdiction of Russia's Asiatic Department transcended the boundaries of the Empire, from Bosnia to Mongolia, and according to Karl von Nesselrode (Foreign Minister, 1816–56) 'fear is the only guarantee, the sanctity of treaties is meaningless, and relationships with those lands belong to the empire's domestic affairs'.

9 The outward flow of Russians was considerable from the late eighteenth century onwards. But until the late nineteenth century, migration policy was full of inconsistencies, thanks to the legacy of serfdom, which made landowners reluctant to 'untie' peasants, the policy of banishment – migration as a form of punishment –

Soviet migration policy, thanks to which by 1989 (the date of the last Soviet census), 25.3 million ethnic Russians found themselves on the territories of what would soon become independent states.

Thus, well before the Bolsheviks turned migration, amalgamation and dismemberment into principles of state-building, borders were a source of insecurity to Russia as well as to its neighbours. The shifting demarcation lines between nationalities and borders always made it possible to argue the case for a greater Russia or a smaller one.

The second legacy is contested national identities. In pre-revolutionary times, as in the present day, identity was shaped as much by historical factors as by the deceptively simple matter of *natsional'nost'* (ethnicity).[10] Belarusians and most Ukrainians shared with Great Russians a common religious faith. But, as Richard Pipes notes, they had also 'been exposed to a far greater extent than Muscovite Russians to Western influences ... [and had] much shorter experience with the three institutions that shaped the lives of Great Russians: patrimonial autocracy, serfdom and communal landholding'.[11] The empire's Polish subjects shared neither a common faith nor that institutional experience.

The autocracy's response to these complexities was both commendably differentiated and appallingly inconsistent – and by turns judicious and brutal. The very notion that the eastern Slav peoples comprised different nationalities with their own histories and identities was anathema, as to a large extent it remains for those who govern Russia

---

and a wariness towards any form of spontaneity on the part of the Tsar's subjects. The famines of 1891–92 were a catalytic moment that encouraged migration to new lands. In 1678, 90 per cent of all Russians lived in the regions that formed part of Russia before the conquest of Kazan in 1552. By 1917, less than half did so. Pål Kolstøe, *Russians in the Former Soviet Republics*, pp. 15, 24–30 (London: Hurst, 1995).

10 Then and now, it is very difficult to establish what 'nationality' means. The first all-Russian census of 1897 asked no questions about nationality, only language affiliation and religion. In the first Soviet census of 1926, respondents were asked about their *narodnost'* (the 'people' they identified with, with an emphasis on *identity*), but afterwards, they were asked to record their *natsional'nost'* (which has a more ethnic and less voluntary connotation). When internal passports were issued in 1932 they recorded the citizen's *natsional'nost'*. Individuals were free to declare the nationality they chose. But the choice then became binding for their descendants. If they were the offspring of mixed marriages, they had to choose one nationality or the other. Ibid., pp. 41–42ff.

11 Richard Pipes, *Russia Under the Bolshevik Regime, 1919–1924* (London: Harvill, 1994), p. 142.

today. Russians, Belarusians and Ukrainians were categorized as Great Russians, White Russians and Little Russians respectively – from which practice derives Vladimir Putin's pointed reference to Ukraine as *malo* (little) *Rossiya* in 2009.[12] But *inorodtsiy* (non-Russians) were treated with greater discrimination. As a subject of the Russian empire, Poland maintained one of the most liberal constitutions in Europe, albeit one that Moscow abridged with growing severity. Finland was afforded a significant measure of self-government until the late nineteenth century, whereas the Baltic provinces (Livonia, Courland and Estonia) were governed under the loyal stewardship of Baltic Germans. Towards the empire's Muslim subjects, who posed no political threat (and offered no model that Russians could possibly emulate), Moscow was relatively tolerant, but only after wars of conquest that were unspeakably brutal. In Christian Armenia (though less so in Christian Georgia), Russia was seen as a protector rather than oppressor.

The third legacy is the ambivalent attitude of Russia's liberals towards the former empire's non-Russian nationalities. Before 1917 liberals and Marxists alike anticipated that economic advance would erode national differences and facilitate assimilation. For Russians preoccupied with Tsarist backwardness and oppression, the national question simply held little interest. Many saw it as a pernicious distraction. On the eve of the revolution, no political party 'was prepared even to contemplate the breakup of the empire along ethnic lines'.[13] The maxim, widely but falsely attributed to George Vernadsky, that 'Russian democracy ends where the question of Ukraine begins',[14] looks back to Alexander II's exclusion of Ukraine, Belarus and Lithuania from his reforms (and the banning of their languages from all printed texts). It also antici-pates the opposition of Gorbachevian 'new thinkers' to the breakup of the USSR and the presumption of dominance that Yeltsin's reformers showed towards newly independent states governed by leaders suppos-edly less enlightened and competent than Russia's own.

The fourth legacy, which by no means pertains to Russia alone, is the use of the national principle as a tool of *Realpolitik*. Vladimir Putin's

12 At a ceremony honouring the White Army General, Anton Denikin. 'Russian PM Quotes White General on Indivisibility of Russia and Ukraine', *Summary of World Broadcasts* (*SWB*), 24 May 2009.

13 Pipes, *Russia Under the Bolshevik Regime*, p. 146.

14 For research on the origins of this expression see http://narodna.pravda.com.ua/culture/4aeg9ccb7daa5a/.

statement that Western 'special services' instigated Ukraine's Orange Revolution was ill-informed, but at least it appealed to precedent. In the decade preceding the First World War, Austria-Hungary financed Ukrainian nationalists on Russian territory, and both the Ukrainian Hetmanate that emerged in 1917, and the Belarusian National Republic that declared independence in 1918 did so under the protection of the Central Powers. For its part, Russian Slavophilism played a role in igniting the 1877–78 Russo-Turkish war and magnified the sense of injury felt when the Germanic powers humbled Russia in the 1909 Bosnian crisis.[15]

The fifth continuity is the obstacle that Russia's internal order placed in the way of its international influence and its control of the empire itself. After the defeat of Napoleon, Tsarist absolutism was a formidable force in Central Europe. Nicholas I, who delivered the crushing blow against Kossuth's revolution in Hungary in 1849, regarded himself as the saviour of Franz Joseph I of Austria, and sought to impose on that country the same client status that his predecessor had imposed upon Prussia. Behind this policy was an outmoded system of power that Nicholas had brought to a state of awesome maturity. The Crimean War put an end to its awesomeness. By then, legitimist solidarity had ceased to define Central European politics. After Bismarck's 'revolution from above', the social and political orders of Germany and Russia seemed decades apart, and neither the pace of Russian economic change after 1890 nor the accomplishments of Milyutin, Witte and Stolypin managed to alter the fact.

Several contrasts with the Bolshevik successor regime should be underscored. Tsarist Russia had no existential idea that could arouse imaginations outside Russia. The belief in Russia's 'universal mission' was confined to Russians and the indigenous elites that the empire had assimilated. Unlike proletarian internationalism, Panslavism was limited in its appeal by definition. Inside Russia, the monarchy and the Orthodox Church had a symbiotic relationship, each strengthening the authority of the other. But this was not true abroad. The Orthodox and Catholic fault line cut across the Slavic world. Panslavism was an idea, not an institutional force. In Central Europe, Panslavists feared

---

15 Dominic Lieven, 'Dilemmas of Empire 1850-1918. Power, Territory, Identity', *Journal of Contemporary History*, April 1999, Vol. 34, Issue 2, pp. 163–200; Norman Stone, *World War One: A Short History* (London: Penguin, 2008).

Russian domination as much as German; the southern Slavs had no enduring love of Russia, let alone one another, and in Russia itself, the Slavic cause was opposed by conservatives in the Foreign Ministry, the army and the court. The coherence of the Russian foreign policy system, and still more the political system, was at best spasmodic. Institutionalization was rudimentary. In its final decades, Russia's security and influence rested upon the power of its armed forces, the skill of its diplomacy and its geographical expanse. In the former respects, it resembled other great powers of the time. The latter afforded no protection against collapse from within.

The Leninist crucible

It was, then, Marxist-Leninist ideology rather than any innately Russian set of attributes that led Joseph Nye to characterize the USSR as the principal competitor of the United States in soft power resources. Yet the foundations of Leninism are as much Russian as Marxist. It is easy to forget that Vladimir Ulyanov became a revolutionary before he became a Marxist.[16] His thinking evolved into a potent amalgam of classical Marxism and revolutionary Populism – and, once war entered the equation, the insights of Carl von Clausewitz.[17] The political liturgy that became synonymous with Leninism – the supremacy of an elite (party) of professional revolutionaries, conspiracy and compartmentalization, a coldly utilitarian approach to the relationship between means and ends, and a single-minded pursuit of power – first appeared in Populist writings in the 1870s.[18] There is nothing intrinsically Marxist about it, and it found little favour with the leadership of the Russian Social-Democratic (Marxist) Party from which the Bolshevik faction split in 1903.

16 Apart from Nikolai Chernyshevsky, other influences on Lenin included the founder of Russian Populism, Dmitriy Pisarev, the Populist-Marxist Petr Lavrov and the maximalist Petr Tkachev, who was 'closer than any other to our point of view'. As Schapiro notes, until the late 1880s 'there was no question of the differentiation of revolutionary circles into "marxist" and "populist"'. 'Liberalism in Russia', pp. 202, 208.

17 For the definitive treatment on Lenin and Clausewitz, see Peter Vigor, *The Soviet View of War, Peace and Neutrality* (London: Routledge & Kegan Paul, 1975).

18 Notably the *Revolutionary Catechism* of 1871 (probably composed by Sergey Nechaev) and the subsequent Programme of *Narodnaya Volya [People's Will]*. Schapiro, 'Liberalism in Russia', pp. 195, 202–06.

Reduced to such terms, 'Leninism and soft power' is an oxymoron. Even its relationship to influence demands elucidation. Yet influence is a central part of that tradition. As Lenin himself wrote in 1920, 'the bourgeoisie sees practically only one aspect of Bolshevism – insurrection, violence and terror: it therefore strives to prepare itself for resistance and opposition primarily in *this* field'.[19] [Emphasis in the original]

By the time Stalin came to power, the Soviet Union not only exercised influence. It had turned it into a science. But the science matured in the crucible of failure. Its cause was the determination of the Bolsheviks to govern alone and by any means necessary. The end and the means became inseparable. The patriarch of Russian Marxism, Georgiy Plekhanov, had warned that a revolutionary *coup d'état* would not create socialism in Russia, only a 'Peruvian tutelage'.[20] By the time of the Kronstadt Rising (February–March 1921), the Bolsheviks had not only declared war against the bourgeoisie, the Socialist Revolutionaries and the Mensheviks; they had also driven some of the most hardened supporters of the October revolution into rebellion. Their tutelage secured victory over all of these adversaries, but the fruits of victory were destitution and international hostility.

Lenin's misdiagnosis of the international situation was neither unique nor altogether flawed. The war, in Marx's words, had 'passed its supreme judgment' not only on the Tsarist regime, but also on the other continental empires of Europe.[21] The perception that the Habsburg lands were ripe for revolution was shared by bourgeois governments. In Hungary, Communists assumed power as the senior partners of a coalition with the support of most of the country. But they lasted five months. Throughout Central Europe, Bolshevik ambitions were thwarted not by imperialism, but by Bolshevik methods and the nativist and national sentiments they awakened. In 1920 those ambitions were reduced to rout outside Warsaw.

The same fate was narrowly averted in the non-Russian territories

---

19 V.I. Lenin, *'Left-Wing' Communism, an Infantile Disorder*, April 1920 (Moscow: Progress Publishers, 1981), p. 85.

20 G. V. Plekhanov, *Socialism and the Political Struggle* (1883), http://www.marxists.og/archive/plekhanov/1883/struggle/index.htm.

21 Lenin was fond of Karl Marx's phrase: 'war passes its supreme judgment upon social organizations that have outlived their vitality'. Eleanor Marx Aveling and Edwar Aveling (eds), *The Eastern Question: Reprint of Letters Written 1853–56 Dealing with the Crimean War* (London: Swan Sonnenschein, 1897), p. 576.

of the empire, where revolutionary forces of different hues had already established themselves. With some willingness to concede autonomy and share power, the new authorities in Moscow might have achieved a pre-eminent position without further bloodletting. But well before Stalin came to power, a different course was set. On the Tsar's historical turf the Bolsheviks had a greater capacity for bloodletting than their opponents. In 1922 Georgia's Menshevik republic was crushed by 100,000 Bolshevik troops (who, in a foretaste of later events, took the precaution of fomenting uprisings in Abkhazia and South Ossetia first). But on alien turf, the Soviets lacked the power to expand the revolution by force of arms. Their misguided attempt to do so helped to revive the interstate system and the bourgeois order of Europe.

As a result, in 1920 Lenin found it necessary to remind his followers, and perhaps himself, that the point was to defeat 'a *more powerful* enemy'.[22] Such a struggle would be protracted; it would demand 'zig-zags', subterfuges and repellent compromises with temporary and 'unreliable' allies. To rule out any such measure 'on principle' would be 'criminal'.[23] Internally, the conclusions were no less profound. '[T]he small commodity producers ... cannot be ousted or crushed; *we must learn to live* with them'.[24] Three years after seizing power, Lenin had entirely reformulated the connection between internal and external policy.

The visible signs of this reformulation were the New Economic Policy (NEP) and the entry into outwardly normal relations with foreign states. What few in Europe saw was that this was a dual-track policy and a dialectical one. The NEP was both a liberalization and a tightening. The Tenth Party Congress, which launched it in March 1921, coincided with the crushing of the sailors at Kronstadt. It banned 'factionalism' in the party and initiated an intensification of repressions against Socialist Revolutionaries and Mensheviks. Even Soviet statistics suggest that the prison population two years after the start of NEP was at least as large as it was before it.[25]

Similarly, few in Europe noticed that the compromise with bourgeois states was accompanied by a tightening of control over the interna-

22 Lenin, *'Left-Wing' Communism*, pp. 9–10. Emphasis in the original.
23 From a chapter suitably entitled 'No Compromises?' Ibid., p. 62.
24 Ibid., p. 29. Emphasis in the original.
25 John J. Dziak, *Chekisty: A History of the KGB* (Lexington, MA: Lexington Books, 1988), pp. 174–76.

tional Communist movement, the virtual sealing of borders and the transformation of the 'Extraordinary Commission' (*Cheka*) into a standing organ of state, the State Political Directorate (GPU).[26] The new policy did not institute normal diplomatic practice, but abnormal diplomatic practice by means of a dual foreign policy whose 'class' component worked to undermine the very states from whom assistance and cooperation were sought. Despite the transparency of the subterfuge, the dual policy, combined with NEP, threw the external and internal enemies of Soviet Russia off balance and severed the connections between them.

By these expedients, Lenin rescued the Soviet state. But at their heart was a tension between influence and control that the regime never resolved and that, until Gorbachev entered the scene, was never seriously addressed. The tension became embedded in the Soviet operational code, as well as in the two institutions that (apart from the party itself) most distinguished the Soviet Union from bourgeois European states.

The more celebrated of these was the Communist International (Comintern), which survived its own dissolution in 1943 and continued under various guises until the dissolution of the USSR itself.[27] In Zinoviev's words, it was to be a 'single Communist Party, with sections in different countries'.[28] Its 'Twenty-one Conditions' not only imposed 'democratic centralism' on member parties but required the expulsion of 'reformists and centrists' from their ranks. In other words, the struggle against the class rival, social democracy (and very soon, Leon Trotsky), took precedence over the struggle against the class enemy. Revolutionary parties that did not agree left the fold in disbelief or anger. Soon a further set of defections ensued. The Sixth Comintern Congress of 1928 enshrined the principle that the first duty of an 'internationalist' was to 'unconditionally defend the Soviet Union'

26 All-Russian Extraordinary Commission for Combatting Counter-Revolution and Sabotage, formally, *Vecheka*. By mid-1921 its Border Troops numbered over 100,000. In February 1922 the *Cheka* became the GPU, in July 1923 the OGPU (Unified State Political Administration). George Leggett, *The Cheka: Lenin's Political Police* (Oxford University Press, 1981), p. 359.

27 In 1943 the functions of the Comintern Executive Committee were transferred to the Central Committee (CC). In 1947 the Comintern was resurrected as the Cominform. At the start of de-Stalinization the latter's executive functions were assumed by the CC International Department.

28 Grigoriy Zinoviev was Chairman of the Comintern Executive Committee (1919–26).

whether or not this defence advanced the international revolution, retarded it or (in the case of the Molotov–Ribbentrop pact) imperilled it. Through these policies, the Soviet leaders acquired a cohesive international instrument and a tool of *Realpolitik*, but in so doing, they lost as much influence as they gained.

The second institution, the *Cheka* (progenitor of the KGB), was organic to the regime from its inception.[29] Its machinery of repression (and that of its successors) is extensively documented.[30] But its role as an instrument of influence is less well known. From the outset, the new authorities needed to understand the forces that might threaten them and, where they could not destroy these forces, divide, beguile and deflect them. The post-revolutionary emigration and the policies of foreign states internationalized this pursuit. The *Cheka* inherited from the Tsarist *Okhrana* a rich tradition of penetrating opposition groups and creating bogus ones. Unlike the *Okhrana*, it built up an extensive *agentura* abroad. This 'agent network' operated cheek-by-jowl with the Comintern, which in operational matters became the *Cheka's* subordinate. Internally, the *Cheka* also built up an extensive apparatus of economic monitoring and management.[31] This was inescapable, because in the 1920s as much as the 1980s, 'speculation' (in other words, private enterprise, corruption and crime) was both a threat to the 'socialist' economy and its silent partner. Abroad, the *Cheka's* international apparatus took on the task of economic penetration and, in order to finance foreign operations, the practice that we now call money-laundering.

Few were gulled by the pretence that the Comintern had nothing to do with the Soviet government. But many influential Westerners were prepared to accept, in the words of President Woodrow Wilson's emissary, that 'the destructive phase of the revolution is over and all

29 The *Cheka* was founded on 18 December 1917, a month before the Red Army. Unshlikht, its ex-deputy chairman, stated that 'without the *Vecheka* and the OGPU, the realization and consolidation of the dictatorship of the proletariat would not have been possible.' *Izvestiya*, 18 December 1927.

30 Between 1865 and 1914, some 14,000 executions were carried out; between 1918 and 1923, at least 200,000: 140,000 by the *Cheka* and Internal Troops. By 1916 the *Okhrana* had expanded to 15,000 officers and troops; the *chekisty* by mid-1921, to 262,000 (Dziak, *Chekisty*, p. 33). Unlike the *Cheka*, the *Okhrana* had no extra-judicial powers or administrative functions and did not run prisons. Leggett, *The Cheka*, pp. 357–61.

31 In 1918 its title was changed accordingly: 'All Russian Extraordinary Commission for Combatting Counter-Revolution, Speculation and Corruption'. Ibid., pp. 222ff.

the energy of the Government is turned to constructive work'. Many also believed that the West needed a new approach. 'We have failed to restore sanity to Russia by force', David Lloyd George declared. 'I believe we can do it by trade.'[32] The strengthening of these perceptions was not only a prime aim of Soviet diplomacy but what would later be called 'active measures': 'overt and covert techniques for influencing events and behaviour in, and the actions of, foreign societies'.[33] Soviet officials, intelligence agents and Western *poputchiki* – 'fellow-travellers' outside the formal party network – were all deployed to this end.[34] Lenin was intent on 'building Communism with the hands of non-Communists'. He found investors who would play their part, as well as 'comrades' who could pose as undiluted capitalists.[35]

The wider strategic aim was to persuade the West that there was no alternative to good relations with Soviet Russia. Apart from attracting investment, this required disorientating Western intelligence services and discrediting *émigré* networks. These ends were facilitated by complex and long-term special service operations of which *Syndikat I/II* and *TRUST* are best documented.[36] By the mid-1920s the West concluded that it was impossible to weaken the Soviet regime from outside and that no credible opposition existed inside, either in Russia proper or in the non-Russian republics of the USSR.

By the time of Lenin's demise, the Bolshevik methods had retarded revolution in Europe. But they created a state that was able to survive without it. They also instituted a singularly subversive form of *Realpolitik* that, by turns, unnerved and suborned the bourgeois world. Before 1917 Lenin would have regarded these results with mordant disbelief. Yet despite the schisms they wrought, these accomplishments earned

---

32 President Wilson's emissary, William Bullitt (later US ambassador to the USSR), whose mission coincided with the founding conference of the Comintern. Similarly, the *New York Times* wrote in 1921 that the Soviet Union 'was getting back to individualism' [*sic*]. French and German business circles echoed Lloyd George, as did Henry Ford, who declared, 'facts will control ideas ... rightness in mechanics and rightness in morals are basically the same thing'. Pipes, *Russia Under the Bolshevik Regime*, pp. 206, 215–17.

33 Richard Schultz and Roy Godson, *Dezinformatsia: Active Measures in Soviet Strategy* (Oxford: Pergamon-Brassey's, 1984) p. 15; James Sherr, *Soviet Power: The Continuing Challenge* (London: Macmillan, 1987/1991), pp. 146–47.

34 Herbert Romerstein and Stanislav Levchenko, *The KGB Against the 'Main Enemy'* (Lexington, MA: Lexington Books, 1989), pp. 35–45.

35 The most celebrated case was that of 'Comrade' Armand Hammer. Ibid., pp. 23–29.

36 Dziak, *Chekisty*, pp. 47–50, 123–34, 147–48; Leggett, *The Cheka*, pp. 294–98.

enormous prestige in left-wing and even some liberal circles, which were impressed by the fact that the 'old order' of Europe had been so convincingly rebuffed. In short, the Bolsheviks acquired soft power.

Alongside it, they acquired influence over politicians and intellectuals with an *a priori* faith in reasonableness, as well as hardened capitalists persuaded that Russia's raw materials could earn them fortunes. Even in countries where communists were shunned by organized labour, 'no group promoted collaboration with Soviet Russia more assuredly and effectively than European and American business communities'.[37] As early as 1920, Lenin concluded that 'muddled thinking' would 'bring about the downfall of the bourgeoisie', and he reiterated this belief with growing conviction before his death.[38]

To its advantage and detriment, the state that Lenin established devised an approach to influence that diverged from conventional practice and matured over time. In the communist world, influence was not divorced from 'hard power' but intertwined with it. Among its most accomplished practitioners were secret services, whose main functions were not intelligence on the Western model, but 'ideological struggle', covert diplomacy, economic penetration and proactive counter-intelligence abroad. Outside the communist fraternity, influence was derived from deception and from the art of mimicking the slogans and pieties of those the regime wished to cajole or destroy. But while Lenin claimed he would 'make use of bourgeois institutions for the purpose of destroying them', he proved more successful at beguiling them, forming a dependency on 'useful idiots' and 'bourgeois muddle' that long outlasted him.[39] Among several reasons the West had for seeking accommodation with Soviet Russia was the belief that doing so would bring 'sanity' to its regime and mellow it. Instead, the regime consolidated its power and built the foundations of what later would be called Stalinism.

The Stalinist codicil

Fortunately, we have no reason to enter the still acrimonious debate about the relationship between 'Leninism' and 'Stalinism'. But a

37 Pipes, *Russia Under the Bolshevik Regime*, p. 215.
38 Lenin, *Left-Wing' Communism*, p. 67.
39 Pipes, *Russia Under the Bolshevik Regime*, p. 186.

paradox needs to be explored. Those who left the communist fold in Lenin's time did so for a variety of reasons. But they never doubted the Bolsheviks' commitment to the cause that brought them to power. By the time Trotsky established his Fourth International, some not only doubted it but concluded that Stalin had traduced the revolutionary cause for the sake of state and personal power. Yet between the launch of Stalin's Second Revolution and the defeat of Nazi Germany, the moral authority and 'power of attraction' of the Soviet state increased. Indeed, the state itself became a focus of admiration. How can this be explained?

For one thing, the new policy line was underpinned by cold political logic. In a world of states, revolutions would be crushed unless they were supported by the power of revolutionary states. For a fleeting moment, it might have seemed that the Bolshevik Revolution would turn 'the whole machinery of state to a museum of antiquities'.[40] But that was an illusion. In 1919 when Béla Kun's Hungarian revolution was crumbling from within, the *coup de grâce* was administered by a Romanian invasion, which Russia's Bolsheviks were powerless to oppose. In 1956 when Hungary's Communists were deposed by an uprising, they were reinstated by the Soviet armed forces, and no other state dared intervene.

What is more, the merits of Stalin's Second Revolution were debated not in an amphitheatre, but in countries confronting the Great Depression and the rise of Fascism. The 'general crisis of capitalism' was not only a communist dogma but an undeniable fact, which gave epochal status to the Five Year Plans and ensured that the Webbs' 1,200-page tome, *Soviet Communism: A New Civilization?* (1935: republished two years later without a question mark) would be treated as social science rather than fantasy. One did not have to be a fantasist to believe that capitalism was in its death throes or to fear that some form of fascism would replace it, and one did not have to be a Marxist to ask whether the communists were the only people capable of opposing its ascendancy. Even many on the left found Edmund Wilson's characterization of the USSR as 'the moral light at the top of the world' dubious, but that is not to say they thought him deluded. Communists were welcomed into the administration of Franklin Roosevelt's New Deal,

40 Lenin, citing Engels, *The State and Revolution* (1918), www.marxists.org/archive/lenin/works/1917/staterev.

and with the onset of Popular Fronts they moved into the mainstream of European political life. Even Trotsky, who had hard knowledge of Stalin's methods, maintained only months before his own murder that the war against Finland was progressive because it would create a workers' state.[41]

The fact is that hardly any of Trotsky's Western disciples, let alone those of the Webbs, had the slightest idea of what life in the Soviet Union was like. If Czechoslovakia was 'a far-away country' full of 'people of whom we know nothing', as Neville Chamberlain said, the USSR was further away and off limits. Credible information was fraudulent and truthful information incredible. Walter Krivistky and Aleksandr Orlov (defectors from the GRU and NKVD respectively) would have done as well to present their testimonies to the Fabian Society as to Western intelligence services. Although the Moscow purge trials provoked considerable shock in left-wing circles, few imagined that beyond those spectacles lay a Moloch's Kingdom in which scores of people could be liquidated to dispose of a rival or meet a deadline.

By this stage, the purpose of Soviet influence operations in the West was not to advance world revolution, but to escape the dangers of a new world war.[42] This new imperative launched a second variant of dual-track policy. Well before Hitler came to power in Germany, it was retooled and reset. Publicly, Soviet diplomats occupied the moral high ground: first by promoting 'total disarmament', then after joining the League of Nations in 1934, by promoting 'collective security'. Yet through covert channels, the USSR pursued very different objectives: an anti-Versailles combination with Germany at Poland's expense. This policy, which emerged even before the 1922 Rapallo Treaty, acquired renewed urgency after June 1934, when Stalin concluded, correctly, that Hitler understood power and would keep it – and deduced, disastrously, that 'state interest' rather than Nazi ideology would govern Hitler's policy.[43]

41 For a concise but evocative retrospective, see Saul Bellow, 'Writers, Intellectuals, Politics' in *The National Interest*, No. 31, Spring 1993, pp. 124–34.

42 On this score, Stalin's 1925 forecast proved prescient: 'Our banner is still the banner of *peace*. But if war breaks out we shall not be able to sit with folded arms. We shall have to take action, but we shall be the last to do so. And we shall do so in order to throw the decisive weight in the scales.' J. V. Stalin, *Works*, Vol. 7 (Moscow: Foreign Languages Publishing House, 1954), p. 14.

43 On the Politburo meeting following the 'night of the long knives', as well as further evidence of this policy, see Dziak, *Chekisty*, pp. 83 –84; Mikhail Heller and Aleksandr Nekrich, *Utopia in Power*, Chs 6 and 7, *passim* (London: Hutchinson, 1982); and W.G.

While the war exposed the full horrors of the Nazi regime, it cast the Soviet Union in a heroic light – at least outside Central Europe. It acquired unprecedented soft power, amplified by allied propaganda. The scale of privation, sacrifice and valour on the Eastern front was reality, not myth, but it entrenched myths and half-truths that to this day are difficult to dislodge. It preserves a distorted picture of how the war began, as well as a caricature of British and French pre-war policy. It displaced memory of the Molotov–Ribbentrop pact: 22 months of *de facto* alliance during which the Soviet industry fuelled the Nazi war machine, communist workers sabotaged allied war production and the People's Commissariat for Internal Affairs (NKVD) turned German refugees over to the Gestapo. It also instilled a lopsided sense of gratitude, for while the USSR broke the back of the German army, had Britain sold out 12 months earlier, its fate would have been sealed. The mythology occluded thought about what 'liberation' would mean for half of Europe and ruled out any consideration of measures that might have mitigated it. Yet within two years of the war's conclusion, the USSR lost its soft power as swiftly as it had acquired it. The West's first Cold War warriors were not Harry Truman and George Marshall but governments of the non-communist left in Europe.

Set against this dramatic record of accomplishment and reverse, the legacy of Nikita Khrushchev is still very difficult to assess. De-Stalinization, the repudiation of terror, the enhancement of living standards and the reconciliation with Tito's Yugoslavia inspired a new generation of Soviet communists, but it also tore the guts out of the international communist movement. In Europe, the suppression of the Hungarian uprising and the erection of the Berlin Wall nipped the potential of de-Stalinization in the bud.

The third incarnation of the two-track policy, 'peaceful coexistence', envisaged measures to avert war coupled with a sharpening of 'ideological struggle' short of war. Yet Khrushchev's policies in Berlin and Cuba brought the world closer to a nuclear conflict than at any time since the Korean War. Less equivocal were the results of Khrushchev's abandonment of the 'two camp' thesis and the embrace of what in 1961 became the Non-Aligned Movement. This dynamic, which derived confidence and momentum from the most repugnant episodes of 'imperial retreat'

Krivitsky, *I Was Stalin's Agent* (1939) (ed. Mark Almond) (Cambridge: Ian Faulkner, 1992), pp. 15–38.

– Suez, the Algerian conflict and the deposing of Mohammad Mosad-degh in Iran – achieved what Stalin had never sought: prestige in the developing world. It was Dwight Eisenhower who pulled the plug on the Suez operation, but it was Khrushchev who got the credit in Africa and Asia. On coming to office in 1961, John F. Kennedy rightly concluded that the theatre of superpower competition had shifted to the developing world and that the West was in danger of losing it.

If the military component of Khrushchev's policy was provocative, it was also deficient. The lessons learned from this 'adventurism' by his successors imposed burdens on the Soviet economy that destroyed the Soviet system. Between Khrushchev's ouster and Leonid Brezhnev's demise, the USSR reached the apex of its global influence and the nadir of its soft power. Yet, paradoxically, in those years the *apparatus* of soft power acquired its greatest institutionalization and scope.

That apparatus could not disguise the fact that the fourth two-track policy, détente, rested on the 'resolute might of the Socialist camp' and little else. 'Stagnation' had begun its cancerous progression even before the crushing of the Prague Spring extinguished any impulse for rejuvenation. Soviet proxy wars in the developing world profited nasty clients and unviable regimes while arousing the apprehension of leaders of standing and significance. Whereas Gamal Abdel Nasser had used Soviet support to strengthen Egypt's sovereignty and influence, his successor concluded that he faced a choice between subservience and a break with Moscow. Whereas Maoist fanaticism had enabled Khrushchev to don the mantle of reasonableness, the prospect of nuclear devastation at the hands of Khrushchev's successors propelled China on its long march to international acceptance and internal transformation. During those years the USSR succeeded at most in persuading certain people that US policy was as dangerous as its own.

Despite these omens, the guardians of Soviet orthodoxy could not see beyond the 'world historical significance' of the US defeat in Vietnam and the 'active measures' campaign that contributed to it.[44] That campaign added tarnish to a US image already tarnished by US policy. It did nothing for the Soviet image. It is not surprising that the West finally launched an offensive against Soviet power and a system that was losing its ability to sustain it. The surprise is that it took a full-scale war in Afghanistan to bring this about.

44 Schultz and Godson, *Dezinformatsia*, pp. 124–26.

The Gorbachevian moment

After 1985 Mikhail Gorbachev not only revived Soviet soft power, but brought it to its apogee. He rejuvenated Leninist methodology in pursuit of aims that orthodox Leninists would have found incomprehensible. He dismantled totalitarianism with the instruments of the Soviet state and employed the Marxist dialectic to renounce the class struggle. But all of this started as a classically Leninist retreat to regain the initiative and achieve asymmetrical results.[45] As we now know, it evolved into a series of improvisations to forestall collapse. The premises, methods and consequences of 'Gorbachev's revolution' matter because they continue to affect Russia and the West.

Gorbachev both reaffirmed and altered the 'very close link between Soviet internal policy and foreign policy'.[46] Perestroika's fate would determine whether the USSR would remain 'a great power or else find [itself] on the margin of history'.[47] It would be instrumental in eliminating the 'stereotype of the Soviet threat' in the West.[48] Yet perestroika and *glasnost'* were also vital for internal reasons: to wrest control of the economy from the 'mafias' that had insinuated themselves into structures of power from bottom to top. The word *glasnost'*, charitably translated in the West as 'openness' but conceived as a tool of exposure and pressure, was originally designed to afford the Communist Party of the Soviet Union a '*much deeper* influence on the state of affairs'.[49] The term, originally invoked by Aleksandr III's adviser, Aleksandr Kireyev, had been embraced by those seeking transparency of society rather than

---

45 Gorbachev forcefully invoked the 1918 Treaty of Brest-Litovsk as an example of 'how short-lived interests could be sacrificed for a historic turn to secure vital interests'. Yegor Yakovlev, *Openness, Democracy, Responsibility* (Moscow: Novosti, 1987), p. 10.

46 Gorbachev declared: 'Our foreign policy is today to a greater extent than ever before determined by its domestic policy.' 'For the Sake of Preserving Human Civilization', *Novosti*, 16 February 1987, p. 7. Evgeniy Primakov (later foreign minister under Yeltsin) said: 'The organic link between domestic policy and foreign policy has never been as clear as it is today', *Pravda*, 10 July 1988.

47 Natalya Dolgopolova and Andrey Kokoshin, 'Lessons Learned From the Destinies of Great Powers', *Kommunist*, No. 2, January 1988.

48 Albert Vlasov, *Mezhdunarodnaya Zhizn'* [*International Affairs*], November 1988, p. 20. Vlasov was Head of the CPSU Central Committee Ideology Department and subsequently head of the Novosti Press Agency.

49 Gorbachev, cited by William Odom, 'How Far Can Soviet Reform Go?', *Problems of Communism*, November/December 1987, p. 20.

the state, and within the state, of lower echelons rather than higher.[50]

On the other hand, perestroika's success depended upon new terms of engagement with the West. At one level, this meant 'demilitarizing' international relations, elevating 'human values' over class values, building a 'strategic partnership' with the United States and a 'common European home' across the NATO–Warsaw Pact divide. At another level, it was a hard-headed exercise designed to replace costly and depreciating geostrategic assets with cost-effective and enduring geopolitical gains. Like Lenin, Gorbachev understood that a relationship based on a mixture of conflict and cooperation would be far more effective than one based on conflict alone. But this did not mean relaxing pressure. It meant changing it. As Khrushchev's rival, Georgiy Malenkov, stated in 1953, 'If today, under conditions of tension in East-West relations, the Atlantic bloc is ridden with internal strife and contradictions, the lessening of tensions may well lead to NATO's disintegration.'[51]

Following this logic, Gorbachev grasped that by 'lessening tensions' – by moving divisions east rather than west, by cultivating right-wing Western governments rather than left-wing peace movements, by praising the Prague Spring and loosening controls over the Warsaw Pact, by seeking to transform NATO rather than destroy it – he would disorientate the West as much as reassure it and acquire the influence that Stalin's paranoia and brutality had forfeited after 1945. This policy ruptured demarcation lines on the left and right, just as it was designed to do. Western governments came under enormous pressure to reciprocate steps that, in their professional judgment, were little more than gestures, including arms reduction proposals that, in their initial incarnations, provided more drama than substance. It is for these reasons that when Gorbachev's spokesman Gennadiy Gerasimov stated, 'we have deprived you of an enemy', he prefaced his words by saying, 'we have done the most terrible thing to you that we could possibly have done'.[52]

In pursuit of these novel ends, the active measures apparatus was not only preserved but expanded.[53] As in the past, it had an overt side

---

50 Pål Kolstø, *An Appeal to the People: Glasnost – Aims and Means* (Oslo: Institute for Defence Studies), pp. 10–16, 44–47.

51 David Dallin, *Soviet Foreign Policy After Stalin* (Methuen: London, 1961/1975), p. 138.

52 Cited in Jonathan Finegold Catalan, 'A Culture of Fear', Ludwig von Mises Institute, 30 August 2010, http://mmises.org.daily/4644.

53 Herbert Romerstein, *Soviet Active Measures and Propaganda: 'New Thinking' and Influence Activities in the Gorbachev Era* (Toronto: Mackenzie Institute for the Study of Terrorism, Revolution and Propaganda, 1989).

(under the Central Committee's Ideology Department, which even in conditions of *glasnost'*, was responsible for mass media), a grey side (under the linear descendant of the Comintern Executive Committee, the Communist Party Central Committee International Department) and a covert side (under the descendent of the *Cheka*, the KGB). But more significant was the change in content. In the words of Vladimir Kryuchkov (later KGB Chairman and co-organizer of the August 1991 coup):

> In the past, we frequently viewed the world in simplistic terms. ... We poorly study and know people ... and we are too sluggish and inconsistent in fighting for their hearts and minds. It is evidently easier to create enemies than to win supporters.[54]

The changes that these insights fostered provoked much disaffection inside the Communist movement. But they did not put an end to malign activity or disinformation. The purpose of the latter, as Kryuchkov well understood, is not to purvey falsehoods, but to provide information, true and false, that is intended to deceive. Because the Soviet Union was at last providing information that was believable, it was therefore believed, whereas internally *glasnost'* was increasingly seen as a cynical exercise.

In the non-Russian republics, the cynicism was even greater than it was in Russia itself. Management of the Chernobyl catastrophe was not only the product of Soviet bureaucracy, whose inner pathologies were exposed as never before, but of an active measures campaign, and the effects of both launched Ukraine on the road to independence.[55] The brutal crushing of protest in Tbilisi and Baku was not the work of an 'old guard' leadership operating behind Gorbachev's back, as the BBC maintained even in 2009, but, as official documents now confirm, the result of 'firm measures' instituted by Gorbachev himself.[56] Few who praised Gorbachev for halting the bloodshed in the Baltic republics

54 *Mezhdunarodnaya Zhizn'*, November 1988, p. 20.
55 Zhores Medvedev, *Gorbachev* (Oxford: Blackwell, 1987), pp. 259–69.
56 As late as April 2009 BBC News Channel upheld the line that 'the old guard leadership sent in troops', http://news.bbc.co.uk/1/hi/world/europe/7972755.stm. Christian Neef, 'Secret Papers Reveal the Truth Behind Soviet Collapse', *Spiegel Online International*, 11 August 2011. According to the same archive of the Gorbachev Foundation, Gorbachev defended the actions in Tiananmen Square at an October 1989 Politburo meeting: 'We must be realists. They have to defend themselves, and so do we. 3,000 people, so what?'

realized that he had authorized it in the first place. It was only *outside* the USSR that he had resolved, in the words of the 1987 Warsaw Pact Military Doctrine, that 'in present conditions the use of force to resolve political problems is impermissible'.

These episodes became monuments to Gorbachev's capacity to deceive the West and himself. Like an earlier generation of Leninists who viewed nationalism as the product of Tsarism, Gorbachev believed that the national cause would dissolve in the currents of reform and democratization. Many Western governments and academics agreed with him. When perestroika turned out to be the catalyst rather than the antidote to national revival in the non-Russian republics, Gorbachev and his Western partners found themselves navigating without a compass. Fortunately, this enhanced prudence on both sides.

The changes that Gorbachev's policies wrought were as much a consequence of his failures as of his successes. These failures were born of a humane impulse. Unlike Stalin, who needed enemies and made them, or Brezhnev, who retained an elemental dread of their influence, Gorbachev believed that the shedding of foreign burdens, the removal of barriers and the overcoming of antagonisms would facilitate the renewal of the Soviet system. In 1968 Brezhnev told Alexander Dubček's politburo that he would have crushed the Prague Spring even at the risk of World War III.[57] By 1989 Western goodwill was more important to Gorbachev than Czechoslovakia was. This calculation, which averted calamity and possibly war, rested on a misplaced faith that the system created by Lenin was 'humanistic' and reformable. It is in a country shorn of this system and these illusions that Boris Yeltsin and his successors have had to reconstruct power and influence.

Conclusion

Countries do not wake up *tabula rasa* in the morning. This does not mean that the continuities of Russian history are cast in stone. They are dynamic ones that produce surprises and make prediction perilous. The dynamic, as described by Vladimir Pastukhov, derives from the fact that Russia has 'dragged unresolved contradictions from one epoch into another, cluttering its historical baggage'.[58]

57 Zdeněk Mlynář, *Night Frost in Prague* (London: Hurst, 1980), p. 241.
58 Pastukhov, *Restoration Instead of Reform*, p. 104.

Long before Putin or even Lenin entered the scene, unresolved contradictions had created a set of security 'needs' out of kilter and scale with those of most European powers. These needs issued from an amalgam of factors that operated in malign reinforcement: the absence of clear physical or ethno-national frontiers; a culture (or 'civilization') that was distinctive and proud, but neither self-sufficient nor self-assured; and a politico-administrative structure equated with stability despite growing signs of its infirmity.

From these factors, several postulates acquired authority: that widening defence perimeters would limit threats rather than expand them, that security was best achieved by instilling fear in others, that one should learn from more advanced powers but not be influenced by them, and that reform and retrenchment should proceed in tandem.

As this chapter has shown, specific approaches to influence emerged as well. Yet it is worth reiterating that many of the techniques and stratagems widely attributed to the Bolsheviks emerged under the Tsarist dispensation. From this inventory, they subtracted nothing. To it, they added organization, 'scientific' methodology, modern communications and a properly transnational ideology.

Although this progression is easily explicable, there was nothing ineluctable about it. Reflecting on the last two hundred years, even the amateur historian is tormented by counterfactuals. In their different ways, the policies of Alexander II, Sergei Witte and Pyotr Stolypin opened up pathways that in more benign conditions might have enabled Russia to emerge from patrimonialism and, if not converge with Europe, develop in harmony with it. It is more difficult to imagine that the non-Russian parts of the empire could have evolved in the same way, and it is scarcely irrelevant that Russia's state reformers did not wish them to. Russia's liberals and reformers were not doomed to failure, but they failed. Bolshevism was not destined to triumph, but it triumphed, and the rule of Lenin and Stalin had consequences that still constrain the art of the possible in Russia and neighbouring states.

3 Russian Interests in the Post-Soviet Era

'Russia is doomed to be a great power.' – Andrey Kozyrev[1]

The West that contained the Soviet Union and eventually became a partner in reforming it was a product of the Soviet Union. Before the Cold War, the West was a cultural but not a political concept. Its European pillars, Britain, France and Germany, lived in a state of armed peace or war. The United States, which rescued the European system during the First World War, had no wish to be a part of it, and after the conclusion of a flawed and punitive peace, it swiftly withdrew from it. Had there been no 'Soviet threat' after 1945, it might have done the same. With no East, there would have been no West.

It is therefore understandable that those who presided over the USSR's dissolution expected that the distinction between East and West would gradually disappear. Instead it gradually re-emerged. This can be explained by the failings of Yeltsin's reformers and the policies of those who replaced them, as well as by the force of prudence and habit in the West itself.

But there were deeper factors. Long before the West existed, Western civilization existed, and the first years of Yeltsin's presidency exposed the frailty of those committed to securing Russia's place in it. Whereas Foreign Minister Andrey Kozyrev was at pains to emphasize Russia's 'normality', Yeltsin himself was driven to emphasize Russia's 'unique' path as early as October 1992.[2] Despite his end-of-year boast that 'the imperial period in Russia's history has ended', even his most radical

1 Cited in Suzanne Crow, 'Russia Debates its National Interests', *RFE/RL Research Report*, 10 July 1992, p. 28.
2 'We will in no way lead Russia to capitalism. Russia is a unique country. It will be neither socialist nor capitalist, it will be Russian.' Interview with *Argumentiy i Faktiy*, No. 42, October 1992.

lieutenants were psychologically ill equipped to manage the interests of a post-imperial state.[3]

Moreover, the West that emerged from the Cold War was no longer a purely geopolitical entity. Shared values were reflected in business cultures, embedded in a network of institutions and codified in law. They also sustained NATO's 'habits of cooperation' and the military interdependencies that diminished the costs of national defence. For at least two generations, mindsets in Western democracies had been shaped by consensus-building and collective decision-making that aimed to reconcile national interests with mutual interests. The civic, political and legal traditions that shaped these mindsets had a much longer gestation.

Russia's determination to evolve in this direction was proclaimed, but its ability to do so was anything but certain. As T. S. Eliot had warned, 'mankind cannot cope with much reality'.[4] After August 1991, Russia had to cope with the collapse of the political system, the economic system, the defence and security system, and the state itself. Those who presided over this collapse were not the Soviet establishment's most radical foes but its most radical members. The midwife of their 'second Russian revolution' was not terror but money. Money and the absence of bloodletting meant that they had to govern in co-existence with Sovietized elites that undermined reform and 'new Russian' oligarchs who undermined authority. When bloodletting finally did take place in 1993, its beneficiaries were not liberals and reformers, but statists and great power ideologists (derzhavniki). When money was finally reconciled with authority, it was accomplished not by Yeltsin but by Putin and on an illiberal basis.

Little of this could be foreseen in 1991, but enough was foreseeable to dissuade the West from making wholesale changes to its institutional arrangements. Nevertheless, Russia's reformers had been bold, and they expected equivalent boldness. When they spoke of integration, they meant merger. What the West meant was partnership, assistance and 'transition': a process without a conclusion. In Russia, the stance of the country's liberals evoked charges of infantilism.[5] In fairness, they

3 Yeltsin, New Year's Message, 'Russia' Television, 30 December 1992, *SWB* SU/1576 C1/1, 1 January 1993.
4 T.S. Eliot, *The Four Quartets*.
5 It was indicative that even Vladimir Lukin, leader of the unmistakably liberal (but

had an exuberant and naïve expectation of what the West could do without abandoning its responsibilities and common sense. Once the limits of Western intentions became apparent, disappointment bred resentment within reformist ranks, including in Yeltsin himself. A 'rebalancing' of Russia's policy followed and, with it, a partial rehabilitation of older forms of influence that were often unfriendly. To these were added new forms of influence that were not always benign.

The perception gap

The propositions that Russia's foreign policy community put to the West in the early 1990s are worth recalling for two reasons. They illustrate that, while there were serious lines of cleavage between the liberals and their critics, there were important points of agreement between them. They also illustrate the difference between Russia as perceived by Russians and by others. This gap in perception has been a major challenge for both parties. Where the gap has been greatest, Russian influence has been a source of tension. Where others have taken Russia at its own estimation, it has usually gained influence. By summer 1992 four Russian 'liberal' orthodoxies had acquired currency in the West, though within a year they were arousing critical scrutiny:

- The events of 1991 were a 'second Russian revolution' and, unlike the revolutions in Central Europe, of 'tectonic' significance;
- A pan-European security system, incorporating Russia on a full and equal basis, was indispensable to the revolution's success and Europe's own security;
- Russia expected recognition as a 'normal Eurasian great power', pursuing its own interests on the basis of democracy, partnership and 'established rules'; and
- Russia had a 'special responsibility ... conferred by history ... and its status as a great power' to strengthen 'centripetal processes' in the Commonwealth of Independent States (CIS), to the benefit of Eurasian integration and security.[6]

---

externally cautious) Yabloko party, charged Yeltsin's lieutenants with 'infantile pro-Americanism'.

6 Andrey Kozyrev, 'Russia: A Chance for Survival', *Foreign Affairs*, Vol. 71, No. 2, June 1992, pp. 1, 11–13. 'Address by Andrey Kozyrev Before the Russian Supreme Soviet', 22 October 1992, in Zbigniew Brzezinski and Paige Sullivan (eds), *Russia and the*

Russia's 'second revolution'

At one level, the new leadership's revolutionary credentials were beyond question. The USSR had been replaced by fifteen new states whose emergence was not forcibly opposed and whose juridical independence was recognized by Moscow. The Communist Party of the Soviet Union (CPSU) was dissolved, and the rump Russian Communist Party was excluded from power. Whereas Gorbachev had abandoned ideological confrontation, Yeltsin and his government disowned the ideology that had been synonymous with the Soviet state. The 'command-administrative' system of the economy, which for long had failed to function effectively, ceased to exist.

But, by comparison with Central Europe, Russia's revolution was a halfway house. In Poland, Czechoslovakia and Estonia, new political systems were being built with new elites that had emerged in the struggle against totalitarian systems more recent and fragile than the Soviet Union's own – and on the basis of a civic heritage and a 'European idea' that Russia did not possess. In the Russian Federation, a new political system was being built by the most radical members of old elites. Analogies with Konrad Adenauer's post-war Germany, advanced by Yegor Gaidar and others, were even more misleading. The Federal Republic of Germany was the product of occupation, de-Nazification and defeat in total war. It based its legitimacy on a repudiation of the state that preceded it. The Russian Federation, as the 'successor state' to the USSR, soon began to base its legitimacy both on repudiation of and continuity with its predecessor.

For these reasons alone, the new Russian state acquired an internally contradictory, even schizophrenic character. In the defence and security sphere, Yeltsin's main priority was not reform, but having loyalists in power. When the Armed Forces of the Russian Federation were established in May 1992 on the basis of what his new defence minister called the 'ruins and debris' of the Soviet Army, the group of military reformers that had coalesced during Gorbachev's last years in power was sidelined.

In the intelligence and security sectors, the picture was much the same. Supporters of the August 1991 coup, beginning with KGB

Commonwealth of Independent States: Documents, Data and Analysis (Washington, DC: CSIS, 1997), p. 79.

Chairman Kryuchkov, were removed. But supporters of the Soviet system remained in place. No programme of reform was adopted (let alone debated), and no lustration of personnel took place either in the former KGB, the Ministry of Interior (MVD) or the military intelligence service (GRU).

The unintended consequences of the 'second Russian revolution' were as great as those that had been anticipated. The dissolution of the CPSU – which was at root a system of supervision and control – made state institutions, not to say bodies of regional and local power, more autonomous than they had been before and more opaque to outsiders. The introduction of market economics forced them to generate their own income. *Nomenklatura* privatization – which transformed bureaucratic into financial power – did not force Soviet industrial managers to behave like capitalists, as Gaidar hoped. It enriched a self-regarding and collusive elite. It also unleashed asset-stripping on a massive scale and legalized the criminalized networks that, *de facto*, had dominated much of the economy. Totalitarianism was being replaced not by liberal democracy, but by a growing nexus between politics, business and crime.[7] In Yulia Latynina's view, personal relations were replacing government as such. In part, this state of affairs stemmed from Yeltsin's decision to divide policy-making institutions in order to make them accountable to him alone. But it also stemmed from the introduction of free-market liberalism to a country without liberal institutions or a rights-based, effective legal order.

As they did after 1917, security and intelligence professionals entered the economic equation, but now as players rather than umpires. Their growing prominence stemmed from the partial commercialization of intelligence and defence sanctioned by Gorbachev, from their near monopoly of *spetsinformatsia* (confidential information) and, not least, from the *Chekist* inheritance: the 'struggle against speculation', the penetration of mafias and their 'extensive international links'. As far back as 1988, Kryuchkov had declared: 'Our service has acquired strong positions in the world of business, but it must show itself more effective in its approach to businessmen, on whom depend advanced

7 For three early analyses, see Yulia Latynina, 'The Economy: New Actors, Old Legacies', in Heyward Isham (ed.), *Reconstructing Russia: Perspectives from Within* (New York: Institute for East-West Studies, 1996); Françoise Thom, *Les Fins du Communisme* (Paris: Criterion, 1994); James Sherr, 'Russia: Geopolitics and Crime', *The World Today*, Vol. 51, No. 2, February 1995.

contracts and access to leading-edge technologies.[8] According to the Foreign Intelligence Service (SVR), by 1994 a large proportion of 400 retired KGB generals held positions in banks and joint ventures.[9]

These developments had implications abroad as well as at home. Russia's mega-economic actors had transnational interests and, in some cases, a transnational presence. The fact that Gazprom had 'begun to conduct its own budget, credit, monetary and regional policy' was not simply a problem for Russia.[10] Intra-elite rivalries were transforming Russia's neighbourhood into 'something of a grab-bag that the Russian political leadership dips into for political rather than policy reasons'.[11] The lines between what was state, what was private, what was legal, what was criminal, what was internal and what was foreign had become perilously blurred. By the mid-1990s, Baltic, Czech and German counter-intelligence services warned that the criminalization of Russia's economy and the commercialization of intelligence were becoming issues of national security rather than simply law and order. They also concluded that Russian intelligence activity in their countries was once again on the rise. For these reasons and others cited above, the West gradually lost confidence that the 'new Russian revolution' would follow the course of the democratic revolutions of Central Europe.

Pan-European security

In June 1992, Andrey Kozyrev assured the readers of *Foreign Affairs* that the new leadership 'simply cannot think of NATO as Russia's adversary'. Yet he immediately followed with a 'qualification': not everyone in Russia agreed.[12] In May 1992, two years before NATO even mooted the question of enlargement, Russia's new draft military

---

8 *Deyatel'nost' organov gosudarstvennoy bezopastnosti na sovremennon etape* [*Activities of the Organs of State Security at the Present Stage*] (Moscow, 1988). From KGB documents released by the Gayauskas Commission (Lithuania), cited in Thom, *Les Fins du Communisme*, p. 63.

9 Sherr, 'Russia: Geopolitics and Crime', p. 36.

10 Alexandr Lebed (then Secretary of the Russian Federation National Security Countil), cited in Stephen J. Blank, *Towards the Failing State: The Structure of Russian Security Policy* (Camberley: Conflict Studies Research Centre, F56, November 1996), p. 3.

11 Markian Bilynskyj, *Update on Ukraine* (Newsletter of the US–Ukraine Foundation), 26 September 1996.

12 Kozyrev, 'Russia: A Chance for Survival', p. 15.

doctrine presented a worst-case analysis of potential enemies and their capabilities. While no names were mentioned, even the undiscerning reader could see that US and NATO armed forces remained the baseline for Russian 'defence sufficiency'. The 'new' army envisaged by the doctrine's authors would be a scaled-down version of the Soviet army, designed for full-scale mobilization and general war. Given the emergence of new, ethno-territorial conflicts in the former Soviet republics, threats to the integrity of the Russian Federation and the collapse of the defence-industrial complex, these were not the most obvious conclusions to draw. The official doctrine of 1993 reiterated the main provisions of the draft in more measured terms.[13] The core premise of Gorbachev's 'new thinking' was repudiated: the use of force 'to resolve political problems' was no longer 'impermissible'.

Swiftly, a second qualification of Kozyrev's assurances about friendship with NATO emerged: NATO's role would have to change. Whether this should occur by means of a new pan-European security body, by NATO's subordination to the OSCE or by admitting Russia to NATO's top table was a subject of endless discussion. When it became clear that NATO had more gradual and modest changes in mind, the expectation turned into a condition.

Thus NATO's Partnership for Peace (PfP), formally unveiled in January 1994, was regarded with the utmost irritation. In May, Kozyrev bluntly stated that it 'cannot suit Russia .... our cooperation cannot be the same as that of medium and small European states'.[14] While some NATO members saw PfP as an alternative to NATO membership for former Warsaw Pact countries, many in Russia saw it as enlargement by other means. At the founding conference of the OSCE in October 1994, Yeltsin warned that NATO enlargement would produce a 'cold peace' in Europe. These views were also held by most ordinary Russians. Although NATO's intervention in Bosnia-Herzegovina was mandated by the UN Security Council, 66 per cent of individuals

13 C. J. Dick, 'Initial Thoughts on Russia's Draft Military Doctrine' (CSRC Occasional Brief, No 12, 14 July 1992) and *Russian Views on Future War* (Camberley: Conflict Studies Research Centre, AA26, June 1993); James Sherr, *Living with Russia in the Post-Soviet Era* (Camberley: Soviet Studies Research Centre, F31, July 1992), pp. 119–32.

14 Fearing isolation, Russia joined PfP in March 1994, but only after proposing (unsuccessfully) that it be accorded special status. Mark Smith, *Russia and the Far Abroad: Aspects of Foreign Policy* (Camberley: Conflict Studies Research Centre, F39, May 1994), p. 9.

polled in February 1994 said they would regard a NATO air strike on Serbia as tantamount to a strike on Russia.[15]

This clash of perspectives gradually became a dialogue of the deaf. That former Warsaw Pact countries viewed NATO membership as protection against a renascent Russia was indisputable. But their elemental and transcendental motive was to escape the legacy of the 'grey zone' and anchor their countries in the arrangements, interests and values into which, by 1994, Russian 'centrists' were saying they had no wish to 'dissolve'. Among the NATO members, not one viewed enlargement as a means of containing Russia; all viewed Russian apprehensions as grounds for caution. For most, but particularly for Germany, the first motive was to prevent the 'renationalization' of defence in new, brittle and immature democracies. The equally strong motive was fear of US withdrawal from Europe's security arrangements and the return of the 'German problem' in national psyches if not in fact. In the end, NATO gave these considerations precedence over Russian interests.

A 'normal' great power

What defines a normal great power is impossible to state with precision. When Britain intervened in Suez in 1956, to the fury of the United States, it did so on the premise that a great power was one that did not need the permission of others to defend its national interests. Great power status has also implied 'special responsibility'. As a superpower, the United States has often claimed a responsibility to uphold international order – and when the USSR was a superpower, it maintained that it had a special responsibility to replace an unjust international order with a just one. In the pre-1914 world, a great power also had the right to limit the sovereignty of others. These definitions are not mutually exclusive, and none of them are highly altruistic. They also dodge a key question about power: does it reassure or alarm others? In Central Asia and Armenia after 1991, it was the swift *diminution* of Russian power that aroused apprehension. But in the former Warsaw Pact countries, in Georgia and Azerbaijan, Moldova, Ukraine and the Baltic states, the opposite was the case.

Since 1991 Russia has claimed great power status in all three respects cited above. The West recognized it in the first sense. The NATO–Russia

15 *Izvestiya*, 5 February 1994.

Founding Act of May 1997 stated that its provisions 'do not provide NATO or Russia, in any way, with a right of veto over the actions of the other nor do they infringe upon or restrict the rights of NATO or Russia to independent decision-making and action'.

But the West has never recognized Russia's great power status in the other two senses. The same text went on to declare that the act's provisions 'cannot be used as a means to disadvantage the interests of other states'. Yeltsin's February 1993 appeal for the 'UN and other leading states' to 'grant Russia special powers as guarantor of peace and stability ... on the territory of the former USSR' was answered with a resounding silence.[16] By that time, a number of 'leading states' had come to suspect that Russia's principal aim in the former Soviet Union was not stability but influence, and while it would contribute to stability where its interests required (e.g. in Tajikistan), it would also, if necessary, secure influence by means of destabilization (e.g. in Moldova or Georgia). While Russian liberals opposed using force for such purposes, their leading exponents argued that Russia must remain 'leader of stability and military security on the entire territory of the former USSR'.[17]

The West's increasing willingness to bypass Russia in its relations with other states in Central Europe, the Balkans or the former Soviet Union produced a marked change in Russian discourse as early as 1993. Kozyrev warned that Russia would not leave those regions that for centuries it had considered its spheres of interest. He later attempted to disown his remarks, yet his language was already enshrined in official policy. The April 1993 Concept on Foreign Policy described the former Warsaw Pact states as a special sphere of interest.[18] The theme was reiterated during Kozyrev's tour of Central Europe in February 1994. In the same month Yeltsin's spokesman Vyacheslav Kostikov stated that 'Russia increasingly sees itself as a Great Power, and it has started saying this loudly'.[19]

16 On 28 September 1993 Foreign Minister Kozyrev declared at the UN General Assembly, 'no international organization or group of states can replace our peace-keeping efforts in this specific, post-Soviet space'.

17 Deputy Foreign Minister Fedor Shelov-Kovedyayev, *Strategiya i taktika vneshney politiki Rossii v novom zarubezh'ye* [*Strategy and Tactics of Russian Foreign Policy in the New Abroad*], pp. 2 and 4, September 1992 [author's copy]. Like Yeltsin, who personally commissioned his report, he also argued that the West should be persuaded to support this 'vital' Russian interest.

18 *Nezavisimaya Gazeta*, 29 April 1993.

19 Kostikov, *Trud*, 22 February 1994.

Special responsibility in the 'near abroad'

While denounced by *derzhavniki* for surrendering Russia's interests to the West, Kozyrev had stated as early as July 1992: 'Entry into the traditional international community ... will not be successful and sufficient for us if we are unable to create a real community of former Soviet republics.'[20]

The rancorous dispute between liberals and their critics was not about whether this 'community' should be created, but how. Some liberals gave every impression of believing that 'centripetal, unifying trends' would emerge among the former republics without any extraordinary effort on Russia's part. In the words of Yeltsin's close associate, Gennadiy Burbulis, 'there is a logic that will bring them back again our way'.[21] This 'logic' was defined by the stark interdependencies of the USSR, by the prominence of the Russian diaspora in many new states and by the power wielded by entrenched, Soviet-era elites. On three points, liberals were of one mind. First, integration of the CIS was a vital interest both in its own right and in order to prevent conflict spreading into Russia. Second, CIS integration and integration into the West were complementary projects that Russia would lead on behalf of all. Third, the principal motor of reintegration would be Russia's internal reforms. In the summer of 1992 First Deputy Foreign Minister Fedor Shelov-Kovedyayev noted all three of these points. Less sanguine than Kozyrev and Burbulis, he saw a need for 'divide and influence' tactics and a 'firm and coordinated policy', but like other liberals he drew the line at military force.

Seasoned members of the old Soviet establishment found this framework and its implicit trust in the West naïve. With 600,000 troops in the former Soviet Union at the start of 1992, the armed forces found it beyond their comprehension. In recognition of these realities, the new Foreign Ministry 'concept' stated that Russia would 'vigorously oppose the politico-military presence of third countries in the states adjoining Russia' and would act to ensure 'the provision of strict observation ... of human and minority rights, particularly of Russians and the

20 *Izvestiya*, 24 July 1992.
21 He added, 'Europe will not take them as they are.' Cited in John Lough, *The Place of Russia's 'Near Abroad'* (Camberley: Conflict Studies Research Centre, F32, January 1993), p. 13.

Russian-speaking population.[22] [Emphasis added] Further, security would depend on Russia's 'ability to uphold with conviction, and in extreme cases with the use of force, the principles of international law ... and to achieve firm good-neighbourliness.'[23]

On 26 April 1994, in a speech to the SVR, Yeltsin declared: 'There are forces abroad that would like to keep Russia in a state of controllable paralysis. ... Ideological conflicts are being replaced by a struggle for spheres of influence in geopolitics.' He did not neglect the economic component, adding that 'Guaranteeing access to other countries markets is an important task both for foreign policy *and the intelligence service*'.[24] [Emphasis added]

One month later, in a speech to the SVR's counter-intelligence analogue, the Federal Counter-Intelligence Service (FSK – soon to become the FSB), he invoked the proactive counter-intelligence traditions of the *Cheka*. 'The main rule' for Russian counter-intelligence was that 'any action capable of damaging national interests should be prevented or neutralized'. Yeltsin added:

> Armed conflicts near Russia's borders are a direct threat to Russia [and] there is vast scope for action for you here. ... The FSK's extensive possibilities must be effectively used in the defence of Russians *both in this country and abroad.*[25] [Emphasis added]

For good measure, Yeltsin demanded that the FSK have 'the right to conduct intelligence operations on the territories of foreign countries', and in April 1995 this principle was enshrined in law.[26] In his last interview as Chairman of the SVR, Yevgeniy Primakov stated that the service was using 'all possible means [to] strengthen centripetal processes' in the former USSR.[27] On succeeding Kozyrev as foreign

22 *Kontseptsiya Vneshney Politiki Rossiyskoy Federatsii*, [*Foreign Policy Concepts of the Russian Federation*], December 1992, p. 2.

23 Ibid., p. 4.

24 ITAR-TASS, cited by *SWB*, 27 April 1994.

25 Speech to the Federal Counter-Intelligence Service (FSK), 26 May 1994.

26 Law 'On the Bodies of the Federal Security Service', 12 April 1995. According to Sergey Stepashin, then Director of the FSB, the law 'brings us into line with what we have been doing for the past year'. ORT (Russian Public Television), 13 April 1995, *SWB*, 17 April 1995.

27 Although, at the time, activity of the SVR in the former USSR was prescribed by law. *Komsomol'skaya Pravda*, 26 December 1995.

minister in January 2006, Primakov described the strengthening of these processes as Russia's highest foreign policy priority.[28]

Thus the policy record does not support the view that a significant change in course arose only after Putin came to power. That the sea change was gradual does not make it insignificant. Russia's liberals lost ground from the moment they acquired it. The progression from a policy that equated Russian and Western national interests to one that juxtaposed them was under way by the end of 1992; by mid-1994 these interests were being expressed 'firmly and in a tough manner'.[29] By 1998 the US government had concluded that Russian policies over non-proliferation and Iran were becoming adversarial and dangerous. Issues that have provoked discord in the Putin era – NATO and EU enlargement, spheres of influence, intelligence methods of business and the use of energy and compatriots as geopolitical tools – arose in the Yeltsin era.

But in two respects, the Yeltsin and Putin eras are sharply demarcated. In the early 1990s Western and Russian liberals believed that Russia's democratization was the key to a harmonious relationship. Many acted 'on the premise that Russia was going to Europeanize like a great Poland'.[30] These expectations had two unfortunate consequences. They left the West unprepared for the liberals' distinctly illiberal policy in the near abroad and their resentment of Western policy there. They also instilled the notion that Russian democracy was the West's business. The warning of Vladimir Lukin, leader of the liberal party Yabloko [Apple], in February 1994 was prophetic:

> There is a firm opinion that America won the Cold War and that Russia lost, and now America has to ... dictate its terms. ... If the United States does not relinquish this tendency of trying to teach us ... no good will come of it.[31]

In the same month Yeltsin felt he had to remind his partners that 'Russia is not a guest in Europe, but an equal participant'.[32]

28 'Zapis' Press-Konferentsii Ministra Inostranniykh Del Rossii E.M. Primakova' ['Transcript of press conference'], 12 January 1996.
29 Yeltsin's address to the Federal Assembly, 24 February 1994.
30 Françoise Thom, 'La politique étrangère de la Russie' ['The Foreign Policy of Russia'], *Commentaire*, No. 139, Autumn 2012.
31 *Izvestiya*, 5 February 1994.
32 SWB SU/1931 S1/7, 25 February 1994.

Second, the key theme of the Yeltsin era was 'multi-voicedness' (*mnogogolosiye*). As Stephen Blank wrote in 1996:

> Even where consensus exists: e.g. NATO should not expand, the CIS must be dominated by Russia, and friendship with China is essential; real policy arises out of the activities of uncoordinated private, factional or institutional groups pursuing their own aims with no concern for a greater Russian national interest.[33]

It was this deficiency that Putin sought to remedy from Day One.

The ascendancy of Putin

The principal distinction between Putin and Yeltsin lay in their respective approaches to the inescapable reality of the 1990s: Russia's insufficiency of means. Yeltsin spoke of 'reconstituting Russia's statehood', but Putin reconstituted the state. During the 1990s, Russia bore less resemblance to a state than to an arena in which powerful interests competed for wealth and power, often at the country's expense. Putin reversed this process, not by renationalizing the economy but by diminishing the relevance of the distinction between state and private, and by recasting the relationship between politics, business and crime on the state's terms. That he did many of these things with the help of liberal economic advisers and adopted many of their flagship causes – flat taxes and deregulation of small business – deflected many Western observers from the essence of his policy: 'the revival of a great state'. With the arrest of Mikhail Khodorkovsky in 2003, the state became greater. Putin became less popular in the West but more popular in Russia.

By these means Putin inverted the relationship between internal and external policy that he had inherited. During the Gorbachev era and the first half of Yeltsin's presidency, Russia sought to create the international conditions necessary, in Eduard Shevardnadze's words, 'to bring about change inside the country'. Putin reverted to the pattern established by Stalin. By means of change inside the country, Putin would restore Russia to its rightful position as a 'great power'.

33 Stephen J. Blank, *Towards the Failing State: The Structure of Russian Security Policy* (Camberley: Conflict Studies Research Centre, F56, November 1996), p. 2.

After more than a decade of Western involvement in the intricacies of Russian democracy and reform, internal policy once again became 'Russia's business'.

Unlike Yeltsin, Putin was a professional *chekist*. As such, he was acutely conscious of power relations and ruthlessly 'pragmatic': a term which the Western mind equates with reasonableness, but the *chekist* equates with the 'strict promotion of national interests' and a coldly utilitarian approach to the relationship between ends and means.[34] Putin also perceived that Yeltsin had left Russia in a very vulnerable position. The vulnerability was underscored by two developments. The first was NATO's 'humanitarian intervention' in Kosovo (seen as a flag of convenience for breaking up 'problematic states' and a testing ground for future variants of 'coercive diplomacy' on Russia's doorstep). The second was NATO and EU enlargement (seen as a means of isolating Russia, de-legitimizing its interests and diminishing its role in European markets). Whereas Yeltsin had responded to these developments with the indignation of a friend who had been wronged, Putin brought to bear all the Leninist disciplines for dealing with 'a stronger enemy'.

Some of these were quite candidly expressed in the 28 June 2000 Concept of Foreign Policy.[35] In the words of Sergey Ivanov (Secretary of the Russian Federation Security Council (RFSC) and a fellow *chekist*), the Concept 'better conforms to the general capabilities and resources of this country'.[36] In the West, where Russia's capabilities and resources were weak, this formulation was seen as reassuring. But in the newly independent states, where these capabilities were strong, it suggested toughness.

The anxieties of Russia's neighbours were borne out by the three objectives that the Concept articulated:

- 'joint efforts towards settling conflicts in CIS member states ... particularly in combating international terrorism and extremism';
- 'serious emphasis on the development of economic cooperation, including ... joint rational use of natural resources';

34 In foreign policy pronouncements, the word 'pragmatic' was invariably coupled with words like 'cold' and 'tough', e.g. ORT (state TV), 18 April 2000: 'Kyiv is sure that from now on Russian–Ukrainian relations are going to be on a much tougher and more pragmatic footing than before'.
35 Published on 7 July; in English in *SWB*.
36 RFSC Secretary Sergey Ivanov, 28 March 2000.

- a determination to 'uphold in every possible way the rights and interests of Russian citizens *and compatriots* abroad', to 'popularize the
  Russian language' and to ensure 'preservation and augmentation of
  the joint cultural heritage in the CIS'.[37] [Emphasis added]

Over the following years, four changes of circumstance enhanced
Russian optimism with respect to these priorities as well as the aim
of securing 'equitable and mutually advantageous partnership' with
the West. The first of these was the rise in global energy prices from
2003, which consolidated the shift in emphasis from geopolitics to
geo-economics. The second was a consolidation of the special relationship with Germany, underpinned by a reinvigoration of industrial and
energy cooperation.

The third was the attacks of 11 September 2001. Putin immediately
grasped that the 9/11 tragedy had changed the coordinates of world
politics, and he rose to the occasion. But whereas the West viewed
these changes with foreboding, he viewed them as an opportunity.
It was the West that now needed Russia. Confident that this was so,
Putin prevailed against internal opposition over the stationing of US
military forces in Central Asia. He resumed cooperation with NATO
(while maintaining his opposition to NATO enlargement), and warmly
embraced British Prime Minister Tony Blair's initiative to establish
what became the NATO–Russia Council. Yet in return, he expected
major political trade-offs. With fair justification, he assumed that the
West would turn a blind eye to his suppression of 'Islamic extremism'
in the North Caucasus, which is juridically part of Russia. With little
justification, he assumed that it would acquiesce in Russia's dominance
over newly independent states, which, in the eyes of international law,
are fully sovereign entities.

The fourth change was recovery from the hardships of the 1990s. At
the start of that decade, the alternative to the discredited Soviet model
was the successful Western model. By its end, large numbers of ordinary
people had concluded that it could only succeed in the West. Sadly,
realities bore out some earlier premonitions about Western policy:

---

37 Welcoming approval of the draft Concept by the RFSC on 24 March, Putin claimed
that it would defend 'the interests of our compatriots ... more attentively, in a more
balanced way and at the same time more aggressively'.

> The greatest danger is not ... that we deny Russia aid and disillusion her, but that we assist her and disillusion her, convincing her people, not for the first time in Russian history, that Western models and values are irrelevant, if not downright harmful, to their peculiarly Russian circumstances and predicaments.[38]

By the end of Putin's first term, Russia seemed to be firmly on the path to an alternative model. Unlike that of the Gorbachev years, this model promised success. Unlike that of the Yeltsin years, it was intrinsically Russian. Its first component was a new, post-Soviet class: moneyed, self-confident, impressed by the virtues of a strong state, uncowed by the West and totally without nostalgia for communism. This class was emphatically European, but it was not liberal. It derived confidence from a state policy that emphasized pride, power, business and the need to compete in a tough and duplicitous world. Its second component was 'the mentality of Russians':[39] ordinary Russians who either retained – or after the 1990s recovered – a primordial fear of disorder and a belief that Russia 'should be a strong state, a capable state, effective'.[40] Its third component was seven per cent year-on-year economic growth, the return of economic stability, the payment of salaries and pensions and the restoration of services and infrastructure.

Crisis and recovery

In late 2004, not only this model but the whole *schéma* of Putin's policy seemed endangered. Ukraine's Orange Revolution was a shock to the mindset and metabolism of Russia's entire elite. In Putin's orthodoxy, Russia 'cannot live according to the *schéma* of Western values'. That Poland and Estonia can do so means little to most Russians. But if Ukraine can do so, that is a different matter. In the dominant Russian perception, Ukrainians are a branch of the Russian people. They are also 'little Russians', and Russia is *starshiy brat* (older brother). Putin has never concealed these convictions. They persuaded him that the Orange Revolution was not the work of Ukrainians, but a Western

---

38 James Sherr, 'Living with Russia in the Post-Soviet Era', *The National Interest*, Spring 1992 (republished in revised form by the Soviet Studies Research Centre, RMA Sandhurst, July 1992).

39 Putin, 'Russia at the Turn of the Millennium'.

40 Vladimir Putin, BBC Breakfast with Frost, 5 March 2000.

'special operation' and a triumph of Western soft power, which to Putin is a form of state power. From 2005, Moscow proceeded to add 'soft power' to its policy toolkit. The perceived later 'failure' of the Orange Revolution was no less significant than its occurrence, because it appeared to vindicate long-held convictions about the 'distinctiveness' of former Soviet space.

When added to the West's reverses in Iraq and embroilment in Afghanistan, that failure fortified resentment with confidence. As Putin said in Munich in February 2007, 'we have a realistic sense of our own opportunities and potential'. He also had a realistic sense that the United States and its allies had become overextended, that NATO's policy in Russia's 'near abroad' lacked teeth and that the alliance was profoundly divided about its future course. NATO hoped that the Bucharest formula – no Membership Action Plans and no timetables, but an existential commitment that 'Ukraine and Georgia will become members of NATO' – would lower the temperature. Instead, it raised it. By then the gap between NATO's aspirations and capability had all the appearance of bluff.

In August 2008 the bluff was called. The Russia–Georgia war had all the hallmarks of a defining moment. Within a single week, it demolished the West's post-Cold War *schéma* of security in the lands between Russia and NATO. It made risible the notion that as Russia became more prosperous, self-confident and economically entwined with Europe, it would abandon its neo-imperial outlook and animus. Not least of all, it overturned Western complacency that Russian hard power could no longer counter Western influence. In Georgia, it not only countered the West's influence but discredited its policy. Its employment, without retribution, against a country enjoying a privileged relationship with NATO held out lessons for other countries, and Russia's state leadership warned of serious consequences if they were not absorbed.[41]

The cadence and substance of policy

As the second half of this study explores, appearance and reality have changed profoundly since the summer of 2008. Yet the themes of

41 At the Valdai Club lunch in September 2008, President Medvedev stated that the Russia–Georgia war had changed the situation in the region and the world. The West had long been 'warned' that it 'did not belong' in 'post-Soviet space'.

Russia's policy towards its principal interlocutors have been notably consistent during Putin's period in office. In each case, its stance can be summed up by a few artfully contradictory propositions.

The 'near abroad'

- Russia's policy in the former USSR is based on the 'impermissibility of force, threats to territorial integrity or political independence'.[42]
- The region is also Russia's 'sphere of privileged interests', built upon 'historically conditional relations'.[43]
- Ukrainians and Belarusians – a 'brotherly people', tied to Russia by a 'common history culture and religion' – have a duty to maintain 'kindred, humanitarian ties', 'tight economic cooperation', the 'unitary' energy infrastructure and joint security.[44]
- Russia will protect its citizens 'wherever they are'[45] and 'considers it legitimate to utilize the Armed Forces and other troops' to this end.[46] It will defend the 'interests' of 'compatriots' and provide them with 'comprehensive assistance'.[47]

---

42 As reiterated in the preamble to the Draft Treaty on European Security , 29 November 2009: *Proekt Dogovora o evropeyskoy bezopasnosti*, http://kremlin.ru/news/6152. Also invoked are the UN Charter, the Helsinki Final Act, the 1982 Manila Declaration and the 1999 European Security Charter.

43 Medvedev's interview with the television company NTV, 31 August 1998, published on the presidential website the same day, kremlin.ru.news. 'Historically conditioned relations' are mentioned in a report by Medvedev's avowedly liberal think tank, INSOR: Igor Yurgens et al., *Russia in the Twenty-First Century: Vision for the Future* (Moscow: INSOR, 2010), p. 19.

44 'Poslaniye prezidenty ukrainiy Viktory Yushchenko' ['Appeal to President of Ukraine Viktor Yushchenko'], 11 August 2009, http://www.kremlin.ru/news/5158.

45 Interview with television company NTV, 31 August 2008. Despite the fact that Medvedev's comments caused a stir, he was restating a well-established policy. The Military Doctrine of 1993 refers to the 'suppression of the rights, freedom and *lawful interests* of Russian citizens in foreign states' as a '*military* danger' [emphasis added]. C.J. Dick, 'The Military Doctrine of the Russian Federation', Conflict Studies Research Centre, RMA Sandhurst, Brief 25, p. 5.

46 *Military Doctrine of the Russian Federation*, 5 February 2010, point 20, kremlin.ru.

47 Vladimir Putin, 'Viystuplenie V V Putina na Kongress sooteestvennikov prozhivauy-ushchikh za rubezhom' ['Speech to the Congress of Compatriots Residing Abroad'], 11–12 October 2001, http://www.mid.ru/bdomp/dip_vest.nsf/99b2ddc4f717c733c32 567370042ee43/c74b760c38b67860c3256b290041b281!OpenDocument. For 'defence' of compatriots, see *Obzor vneshney politiki Rossiyskoy Federatsii* [*Foreign Policy Review of the Russian Federation*], 431, 27 March 2007, http://www.mid.ru/brp_4.nsf/0/3647 DA97748A106BC32572AB002AC4DD.

Post-communist Europe

- The region will be neither secure nor prosperous in the absence of good relations with Russia – NATO and EU membership cannot make Russia disappear.
- Bilateralism retains its traditional force and cannot be wished away. So long as France and Germany have strong ties with Russia, the east-central European states have no choice but to develop their own relationships with Moscow.
- Whereas the EU aims to suppress national identities rather than enhance them, Russia builds its relations on the basis of tangible national interests.
- Only Cold War stereotypes prevent the states of the region from recognizing their distinctiveness from Western Europe and perceiving their historical relationships with Russia in more balanced and favourable terms than they currently do.
- American 'hegemonism' and the myth of 'the West' artificially 'securitize' energy policy and keep economic relationships well below their actual potential.

'Old' Europe

- There can be no European security without Russia. The exclusion of Russia is a Cold War policy, damaging to Europe as a whole.
- The current architecture of security is flawed because it is preserves Cold War dividing lines, bases itself on the preferences of a small group of states and maintains the hegemony of non-European powers at the expense of Europe.
- The EU is not synonymous with Europe. It cannot be the arbiter of human rights outside its borders; 'soft security' is not its proper business.
- Russia's position as an energy supplier is a key element of economic interdependence and meets the interests of all European states. Russia will remain a reliable partner. But it will not accept discrimination on the basis of rules devised by others.
- Russia is integral to European civilization. It supports measures to strengthen Europe's common Christian inheritance, its ethnocultural roots and the modern foundations of nation and state. But it will oppose the pseudo identities of 'the West', post-modernism and multiculturalism.

NATO

- Russia 'is ready to develop relations of partnership with NATO'[48] but is obstructed by NATO's refusal to abandon 'unipolarity', its 'mechanical enlargement', its movement of 'military infrastructure' closer to Russia's borders, its construction of missile defences and its use of force in violation of the UN Charter.[49]
- Atlanticism cannot be the basis of global security. NATO cannot substitute for a pan-European security mechanism in which Russia has an equal and authoritative role. It must abandon its 'civilizational exclusiveness' and confine itself to 'hard security' issues within the 'geographical limits of the alliance'.[50] Isolating Russia damages NATO's own security.[51]

The United States

- Russia seeks a wide-ranging partnership with the United States on issues of global importance: the limitation of nuclear arsenals, non-proliferation of dangerous weapons, counter-terrorism, counter-narcotics, anti-piracy, the war in Afghanistan and collective management of the global financial order.
- The United States must accept multipolarity as a political reality and normative principle. It must act in strict accordance with the UN Charter, it must abandon unilateral approaches, 'coalitions of the willing', and the habit of dictating to others.

Conclusions

On the basis of these formulae and principles, several conclusions can be drawn.

First, Russia respects the sovereignty of its former Soviet neighbours, but it also maintains a right to define what it means in practice. As in

---

48 Dmitriy Medvedev, *RIA Novosti*, 16 November 2008.

49 See *Military Doctrine of the Russian Federation*, 5 February 2010, Point 8, kremlin.ru.

50 Vladimir Voronkov, Director of the Department for Pan European Cooperation of the MFA, cited in Mark Smith, *Russia and the Transformation of NATO*, UK Defence Academy, 11 January 2011, p. 7.

51 Sergey Lavrov, 21 August 2008. The then ambassador to NATO, Dmitry Rogozin, stated that 'the West needs us more than we need it'. Mark Smith, *Russian Domestic Chronology 2010*, UK Defence Academy, p. 5.

the case of the former Warsaw Pact, this 'privileged' sphere observes 'higher norms' than those required by international law. (As Putin admits, compatriots is not just a legal category.[52]) These norms reflect 'kindred humanitarian ties' that have developed over centuries. For the Kremlin, 'tighter integration' is a historical imperative, much as the 'revolutionary process' was for the Soviet Union. In relation to Ukraine, that certainty lay behind Dmitry Medvedev's public 'appeal' to Viktor Yushchenko in 2008, as well as his response ('it is only the beginning') to Viktor Yanukovych's protest against Russian pressures for closer integration in 2010.[53]

These views pose an ideological challenge to liberal democracy. For liberals, the basis of legitimacy is consent, and when consent is strained (as in the eurozone crisis) legitimacy suffers. For Russia and its allies, the basis of legitimacy is 'history', which in the post-Hegelian lexicon describes what has yet to occur.[54] Putin asserts that 'the choice of the Russian people has been confirmed again and again – not by plebiscites or referendums – but by blood'. By this, he is not suggesting that blood is a choice, but the opposite: that blood (i.e. identity) is more important than choice and that 'historically conditioned' relations have greater legitimacy than consent (which can be granted or withdrawn) or the 'notorious principle of national self-determination'.[55]

These views also pose a challenge to international law. They revive the Tsarist and Soviet understanding of sovereignty as a contingent rather than absolute principle, conditioned by cultural inheritance and power. The former chairman of the Federation Council, Boris Gryzlov, has no difficulty stating that the Eurasian Union will function as 'a

---

52 Vladimir Putin, *Viystuplenie V V Putina na Kongress sooteestvennikov prozhivauyushchikh za rubezhom* ['Speech to the Congress of Compatriots Residing Abroad'], 11–12 October 2001; Gatis Pelnens (ed.), *The 'Humanitarian Dimension' of Russian Foreign Policy Toward Georgia, Moldova, Ukraine and the Baltic States* (Riga: Centre for East European Policy Studies, Konrad Adenauer Stiftung, Soros Foundation Latvia, 2nd supplementary edn, 2010), p. 47.

53 'Medvedev: Eto tol'ko nachalo' [Medvedev: It's only the beginning], *Glavred*, 17 May 2010, www.glavred.info.

54 As the former foreign minister of Transnistria, Valeriy Litskai, said to the author in 2008, Moldova could never join the EU because it was never part of the Holy Roman Empire.

55 Vladimir Putin, 'Rossiya: Natsionalniy Vopros' ['Russia: The National Question'], *Nezavisimaya Gazeta*, 23 January 2012 [hereafter 'The National Question']. At the Valdai Club in 2008, Medvedev used similar terms: 'shared, common history' and the 'affinity of our souls'.

single country' made up of 'sovereign states'.[56] Even the prominent opposition figure Alexei Navalny adheres to the view that Ukraine's integration with Russia is a 'natural political process' because Ukraine is weaker and because 'we are one and the same people'.[57] 'Compatriots', too, is an elastic term that, like limited sovereignty, has no legal standing.

Second, Russia does not aim to decouple the two parts of Europe, let alone the United States from Europe. It knows that such an effort is unlikely to succeed. But it does seek a looser, more discordant coupling with a pivotal and recognized role for itself in both the parts and the whole. To these ends, it combines blunt statements of self-interest with a principled advocacy of collective approaches. It is inclusive regarding its own participation in wider European affairs, but in its own presumptive sphere it draws red lines.

Third, Russia regards NATO as a Cold War construct, and its 2010 military doctrine defines NATO's policies as the main 'external military danger' facing the Russian Federation. It remains unreconciled to NATO's place in the world and has difficulty accepting that its more problematic undertakings (e.g. missile defence, the Kosovo intervention and the Libya campaign) are not directed against itself. As Mark Smith has observed, 'Moscow's argument that Atlanticism is obsolete and non-viable is in reality a reflection of its unwillingness to come to terms with the continued existence of NATO in its current form as a collective defence organization'.[58] Because this collective defence is based upon common values as well as common interests, Moscow claims that NATO perpetuates a 'civilizational schism' in Europe that would run along Russia's borders if its neighbours joined the alliance.[59] Whereas NATO believes it has transformed itself by reshaping armed forces to deal with post-Cold War and extra-European challenges,

---

56 Boris Gryzlov (then chairman of the upper house of parliament), Valdai Club, 6 September 2011.

57 'Ukrainskie zhurnalisty obrushilis' s kritikoy na Naval'nogo za predlozhenie ob integratsii Kieva i Moskviy' ['Ukrainian journalists pan Navalniy's proposal for the integration of Kyiv and Moscow'], *Noviy Region* [*New Region*], 11 February 2012, http://nr2.ru/kiev/372311.html.

58 Smith, *Russian Domestic Chronology 2010*, p. 6.

59 Major General Vladimir Dvorkin, cited in Lilia Shevtsova, *Odinochkaya Derzhava: Pochemu Rossiya ne stala Zapadom i pochemu Rossii trudno s zapadom* [*Lonely Power: Why Russia Will Not Become Western and Why Russia Will Remain Difficult for the West*] (Moscow: Moscow Carnegie Centre, 2010), p. 101.

Moscow views Russia's exclusion as proof that no transformation has taken place. Whereas NATO defines equality as the *absence* of veto power over one another's actions, Russia defines it as 'real influence on the decision-making process' in NATO itself.[60] Its response is three-fold: to expand its prerogatives *de jure* by a new security treaty; to expand them *de facto* by dividing NATO and bilateralizing its relation-ships; and to seek to confine NATO to defence against 'hard security' threats in its 'traditional geographic area'.[61] Were these initiatives to be accepted, NATO would lose its autonomy and its relevance.

Fourth, Russia's position toward the United States is broadly consis-tent with American 'realism'. Russia welcomes the primacy of global, post-9/11 security interests (provided the United States acts in accor-dance with the UN Security Council), it supports the diversion of US attention and resources from Europe, it looks for opportunities to show that its partnership is helpful, and it seeks to demonstrate that 'unilateral' approaches harm US interests. But on several global issues, notably Iran and Syria, Russia is not a partner but an obstacle. This is less because Russia is playing the spoiler than because it is a Westphalian power opposed to regime change, and a suspicious power that fears any other stance will help to legitimize US pressure against the Russian regime itself. Nevertheless, the 'unilateralist' stigma that tarred Obama's predecessor is beginning to rebound on Moscow. Over Syria, Russia has not only defied the United States but every other member of the UN Security Council except China. It has also put itself at cross-purposes with the Arab League and Turkey.

---

60 Konstantin Kosachev, 'Three Birds with One Stone?'; James Sherr, 'Doomed to Disappointment?', *NATO Review*, July 2011.
61 Draft Treaty on European Security, November 2009.

4 The Modalities of Influence

'The West comes here to teach lessons; we offer brotherly assistance.' –
Vladimir Putin to Leonid Kuchma, Kyiv, April 2000

Influence is not an entitlement. In or outside a 'brotherly' context, countries rarely get it by demanding it. When Vladimir Putin came to power, Russia's demands for influence corresponded neither to the wishes of others nor to the means at its disposal. Of the many factors that confer influence – interest, attraction, dependency, habit – the most traditional one is national power. It is this that Putin set out to reconstitute, both in Joseph Nye's old-fashioned sense of the term – 'the possession of capabilities or resources that can influence outcomes' – and in his dynamic and relational sense: the ability to 'get the outcomes one wants'.[1] By transforming much of Russia's hitherto privatized energy sector into 'an instrument of internal and external policy', Putin sought to increase Russia's political as well as its economic weight.[2] By the classical employment of hard power – first against secessionist Chechnya in 1999 and then against Georgia in 2008 – he sought to consolidate the Russian Federation and secure the pre-eminence in Russia's 'near abroad' that had eluded him and his predecessor. Even strengthening 'humanitarian' ties and promoting the Russian language was presented by Putin as a way 'to make Russia strong'.[3] From 2003 to the Russia–Georgia war, 'Russia's resurgence' was an appropriate moniker for this process.

Today, in a number of respects, the realities facing Russia appear less favourable than they did at that time. First, converting hard power

1 Nye, *Soft Power*, p. 3.
2 As described in *Energeticheskaya strategiya Rossii na period do 2020* [*Energy Strategy of Russia to 2020*], Government of the Russian Federation, 28 August 2003, No. 1234-g.
3 'Resuscitating Russian', *Transitions Online*, 5 April 2000, http://www.tol.cz/apr00/resus.html.

into lasting influence has not been an easy matter. Russia's dramatic military victory over Georgia has secured no dividends in the North Caucasus. The notional independence of Abkhazia and South Ossetia has not made these statelets viable, nor has it diminished the gravity of threats facing Russia in its southern borderlands. The development of Russia's Armed Forces is itself highly uncertain. Anatoliy Serdyukov's wrenching reforms attacked not only the ills but the bone marrow of the military establishment, and upon replacing him as minister of defence in November 2012, Sergey Shoygu announced their curtailment.

Second, the energy landscape has changed substantially, to the detriment of the major source of Russia's export earnings and a key pillar of its international influence. Unconventional gas, tight oil and new technologies of coal generation are rewriting the rule book in what recently had been regulated and stagnant energy markets, uncomfortably dependent on Russian pipeline gas. While Russia might be able to utilize (or counter) some of these changes to its own benefit, the assumption of growing European dependence on Russian energy now looks vulnerable.

Third, China's self-confidence and power are inescapable realities for Russia, and the limits of 'strategic partnership' with that country can no longer be denied. As the world's second economy and principal energy importer, China has choices and market power. It will not accept either the price structure or the treatment that Europe has long tolerated from Russian suppliers. In Central Asia, China's menu of interests is not designed to damage Russia, but it no longer will be trimmed for the sake of Russian *amour-propre*, and the same is becoming true in the European post-Soviet states. In Moscow, the possibilities of Russia succumbing to 'Finlandization' and becoming a 'raw-material appendage' to China are now openly discussed by sober and influential people.[4]

Fourth, the US–Russian reset has exhausted its limited utility for both parties. Its demise is not a failure. The reset produced useful

4 Council on Defence and Foreign Policy, *Russia Should Not Miss Its Chance*, p. 30. The same study states that 'China will gradually replace Russia in Central Asia, Kazakhstan, *Belarus and Ukraine*' (p. 34, author's emphasis); Speech by Sergei Karaganov, 'Russia's International Role in the Coming Decade', Chatham House, 10 December 2009.

agreements and did no harm. But the menu of mutual interests proved to be far smaller than the menu of common interests.[5] Hope that progress in some areas would generate momentum in others proved unfounded. The START accords produced no impulse for further accords in tactical nuclear weapons or conventional forces. The effort to disentangle values from geopolitical substance foundered in Libya, Syria and Butyrka prison.[6] On almost any issue that attracts attention in the United States, Russia's image is unfavourable and worsening. Most critically, the reset's demise starkly highlights the different stakes attached to the relationship. For Russia, the United States remains the basis of threat assessment and the ultimate standard against which its own power and influence are measured. For the United States, Russia has assumed an instrumental rather than existential importance. After US combat forces complete their withdrawal from Afghanistan, its importance could recede further. The reset did nothing either to alter that fact that in the post-Cold War domains of trade, investment and energy, Russia's influence over the United States is minimal. For all of these reasons, the risk is that Washington will view Russia purely as a problem rather than as a central factor in the management of global affairs.

Finally, the relationship between Russia's political system and its international prestige is no longer a favourable one. Between 2001 and 2008 Vladimir Putin restored not just order to Russia's affairs, but also collective self-respect – and he accomplished both on the basis of prosperity and defiance of Western orthodoxy. Today, the most visible part of this picture is defiance. Among Russia's urban middle classes, the conventional wisdom is that the interests of Russia's ruling elites damage the interests of the country, and this conclusion is now shared by a significant cross-section of Russia's partners and neighbours.

5 The distinction is borrowed from Andrew Monaghan, *From Lisbon to Munich: Russian Views of NATO–Russian Relations*, Research Division, NATO Defence College, Rome, February 2011, p. 2.

6 Sergei Magnitsky, a Russian accountant and auditor whose arrest and subsequent death in custody generated international media attention and triggered both official and unofficial inquiries into allegations of fraud, theft and human rights violations, was imprisoned in Butyrka. Magnitsky legally represented Hermitage Capital, once the largest UK hedge fund investor in Russia, and found himself arrested in 2008 after contesting charges of fraud launched against Hermitage by the Ministry of the Interior. He died of multiple injuries in Butyrka in 2009 after 11 months' detention without trial (and eight days before his legally mandated release).

Yet three other trends provide compensation and opportunity for Moscow. First, while the global financial crisis is also Russia's crisis, its impact on the dynamics of European integration could be far more profound. This sea change in image and expectations has not only provided geopolitical respite for Moscow, but also low-hanging fruit of possible benefit to Russian diplomacy and business in disaffected parts of Europe. Grass-roots support for closer ties with Russia recently expressed in Cyprus may reflect thinking (or its absence) in the heat of the moment, but it is an indication of how greatly the EU's image has been damaged in parts of Europe.[7] The financial crisis has also given impetus and an aura of plausibility to Russia's schemes of integration in the former USSR: the Eurasian Customs Union and the Eurasian Union, which Putin asserts will 'change the geopolitical and geo-economic configuration of the entire continent' and also 'bind Europe together'.[8]

Second, the 'Asian pivot' of the United States must subdue hopes that its withdrawal from Afghanistan will see a redeployment of effort to post-Soviet Europe. Apprehensions that the Arab Spring will be followed by an Islamist winter – ruefully noted in Moscow – must also dampen such hopes. The weight of these concerns might persuade Washington that it would be wiser to accommodate Russia than ignore it. First appearances suggest that Obama's new national security team might have drawn this conclusion, and neither the latest revisions to the missile defence programme (announced in the absence of consultation with Poland or Romania) nor Moscow's warm reaction to John Kerry's appointment contradict this impression.

Finally, the prospect of further NATO enlargement remains as remote as it was after the Russia–Georgia war. Ukraine, Georgia and Azerbaijan – countries that recently regarded themselves as the principal beneficiaries of NATO's model of partnership and cooperation – have begun to ask how far this model advances their core security interests.

Having discussed the ends, we now discuss the means of Russian influence. In the body of this chapter, we set out the four principal dimensions of influence in the Putin era: diplomacy and messaging, business, energy supply and 'humanitarian' efforts (which most

---

7 In a recent TV poll two-thirds of respondents favoured closer ties with Russia over further EU integration. 'Limassol fears for life after Russians', *Financial Times*, 29 March 2013.

8 Vladimir Putin, 'A New Integration Project for Eurasia – A Future Being Born Today', *Izvestiya*, 4 October 2011. *Johnson's Russia List*, No. 180, 6 October, Item 30.

approximate to the letter if not the spirit of soft power). In Chapter 5, we ask whether these means are fit for purpose in a rapidly changing environment.

State and public diplomacy

In view of what has been said thus far, it should cause little surprise that Russian diplomacy preserves many features of its Soviet predecessor. As a rule, it is highly professional. Diplomacy, like war, is seen as a tool of policy and is not to be confused with policy itself. Depending on its aim, it can be cooperative, confrontational, honest or devious. Negotiations are not pursued as exercises in group therapy but as a means of advancing national interests. Agreement is not an end in itself. An impasse is not a stalemate if it blocks undesirable action or prolongs a situation that is only unhappy for others. What has been said about the 20-year Transnistria negotiation process has broader application: 'If a settlement plan that meets is criteria is not on the table, Russia is content with the status quo.'[9] Until Russia felt strong enough to force the issue in Georgia, it was content with 18 years of frozen diplomacy.

Some staple methods bear restating. One is to stake out an uncompromising position and adhere to it. Such a stance may disguise indecision, but it may also expose it on the other side, particularly when that side consists of a number of different parties. When combined with what the late Lord Strang called 'ruthless questioning' and the 'stress of argument', persistence can wear down opposition.[10] By endlessly reiterating the threat posed to Russia's strategic deterrent by NATO missile defences and by 'ruthless questioning', Russia has gradually encouraged NATO experts to find justifications for a proposition that most of them initially found implausible. It has also stimulated ways of bringing Russia into institutional arrangements that once were considered off-limits.

A second method is to create contradictions and use them. Thanks to an elaborate scheme entered into with Gazprom-owned Moldova

9 Nicu Popescu and Leonid Litra, *Transnistria: A Bottom-Up Solution*, European Council on Foreign Relations, ECFR/63, September 2012, p. 4.
10 Lord Strang, 'The Moscow Negotiations, 1939', in David Dilks (ed.), *Retreat from Power: Studies in Britain's Foreign Policy of the Twentieth Century, Vol. I, 1906–1939* (London: Macmillan, 1981), p. 177.

Gaz and Tiraspoltransgaz, Moldova's separatist region, Transnistria, has amassed a debt to Gazprom that is larger than Ukraine's. Yet Moldova has no means of altering these arrangements or exercising sovereignty over this separatist entity, which is part of its territory *de jure*. In the words of Deputy Prime Minister Dmitry Rogozin (who is also the president's Special Representative on Transnistria), 'If Moldova will not recognize Transnistria, then it means that the gas consumed by Transnistria ... is Moldova's debt, and Moldova should pay for it.'[11] By this logic, Moldova would assume responsibility for a system that Russia has created despite its objections.

A third diplomatic method is to leverage such gambits against others. In November 2012, Rogozin signalled that he would delay a new gas contract for Moldova unless Chisinau consented to the establishment of a general consulate in Transnistria's capital, Tiraspol.[12] Yet there is no suggestion that Chisinau's consent will resolve the debt issue, which can be revived at any time of Moscow's choosing.

Russian public diplomacy has its own syntax and idiom. It produces a stream of analogies that only the expert would find spurious. Thus, the Eurasian Customs Union and Eurasian Union are presented as equivalent to the European integration process (and the Collective Security Treaty Organization (CSTO) as equivalent to NATO) despite significant dissimilarities in ethos and in the way they function. As noted in a recent Moldovan study:

> Moldova gets substantial grants and credits [from the West], which are mostly invested in development, such as roads, irrigations systems and institution building ... In contrast, virtually all Russian assistance to Transnistria is spent on current spending with little developmental potential. And unlike Western aid ... very little [of it] can be audited.[13]

Russia hands out passports to its compatriots abroad, but, as Putin often remarks, so does Romania (even though Romania's purpose is not to undermine Moldova, but to facilitate visa-free access to the EU

---

11 Popescu and Litra, *Transnistria*, p. 5. As the authors point out, '[t]he money collected from gas consumers in Transnistria is not transferred to Moldova Gaz and Gazprom, but instead is spent by the secessionist authorities'.

12 Dumitru Minzaran, 'Russia's Aggressive Policies in Transnistria Reveal Severe Limitations of EU's Approach to Conflict Resolution', *Eurasia Daily Monitor*, Vol. 9, Issue 210 (Washington, DC: Jamestown), 15 November 2012.

13 Popescu and Litra, *Transnistria*, p. 6.

for its citizens). Russia seeks a sphere of influence in the former USSR, but what about the Monroe Doctrine? Russia's war in Chechnya is analogous to the US Civil War and Canada's struggle against Québec separatist paramilitaries.[14] Gazpom is run by the state, but what about Statoil (whose corporate governance insulates it from political interference)? Balts and Ukrainians who fought against the Soviets are 'Fascists' whether or not they fought the Nazis as well. Chechen fighters are 'terrorists' whether they target non-combatants or not. Those who seek to strengthen Ukrainian identity are 'aggressive nationalists' whether their national ideas are ethnic, cultural or civic. 'Russophobia, like anti-Semitism, is a manifestation of aggressive nationalism.'[15]

Alongside such analogies are magisterial banalities and quarrels with straw men. The statement that 'all countries have national interests' is as true (and as meaningless) as the statement that all people drink. What are Russia's interests exactly? 'Russia has no wish to restore the Empire.' But what does it wish to do instead? Are Belarus and Ukraine parts of a former empire or parts of greater Russia? Russia only seeks 'soft domination' in its neighbourhood. But how significant is that if, as in Georgia and Moldova, coercion is used to achieve it?[16] Mixed messages are also prominent. Sergey Lavrov believes that 'national egotism' should be removed from economic relations in favour of a 'genuinely collective approach', but he also believes that Russia's business advances its 'foreign policy potential' and that its positions abroad should be 'enhanced'.[17] Dmitry Rogozin insists that NATO missile defences 'will not be effective against Iranian missiles'.[18] Yet he, like the Kremlin and Ministry of Defence, asserts they pose a threat to Russia's deterrent.

Mixed messages and skewed analogies are tools of manipulation. But they also reflect genuine differences about the meaning of terms

14 According to defector Sergey Tretyakov, these specific analogies were conceived by the SVR and then propagated by Western officials. Pete Earley, *Comrade J: The Untold Secrets of Russia's Master Spy in America After the End of the Cold War* (New York: Berkley Books, 2007), pp. 167ff.

15 Deputy Foreign Minister Vitaliy Churkin (1994), cited in L. Yermakova, 'Churkin says protection of Baltic Russians "priority"', ITAR-TASS, 6 March 2012, http://data.synthesis.ie/site_media/trec/FBIS/FB1S3-15498.txt.

16 Dmitri Trenin, *Post-Imperium* (Washington, DC: Carnegie Endowment, 2011), p. 81.

17 Sergey Lavrov, 'Diplomatiya i biznes' ['Diplomacy and Business'], *Mezhdunarodnaya Zhizn'*, 6 April 2004.

18 Chatham House roundtable, 2009.

and motivations of others. Brussels claims that 'the EU neither seeks a sphere of influence, nor will it recognize one'.[19] Were this not true, it would be difficult to explain the EU's rebuff of overtures from Belarus for closer ties or its shelving of an Association Agreement with Ukraine. Yet this does not diminish the perception of many in Russia that the EU is engaged in a 'fight' for a sphere of influence in the former USSR, 'disguised in parables about democracy'.[20] Many also perceive that the United States 'needs the perceptions of antagonism [with Russia] to justify international and even domestic policy'.[21] But this is not a portrait that most Americans would recognize. The war in Kosovo disposed of the notion that NATO is a 'strictly defensive alliance'. But no participant in that undertaking would agree that 'today they are bombing Yugoslavia but aiming at Russia'.[22] Nevertheless, this conviction led to a toughening of Russian policy throughout the Caucasus. In sum, the enlargement of NATO, the abrogation of the Anti-Ballistic Missile Treaty and the wars in the Balkans reinforced the belief that 'partnership' with the West is a mug's game, and Moscow plays accordingly.

Instruments of influence

Like their Soviet predecessors, Russia's authorities have developed a proclivity for instrumentalizing that which governments in liberal polities control with difficulty or not at all. The first paragraph of Russia's 2003 energy strategy defines the 'mighty energy sector' as an 'instrument for the conduct of internal and external policy'.[23] Culture is defined in almost identical terms – as 'an instrument to ensure Russia's economic and foreign policy interests and positive image in the world'.[24] The authors of the state-supported 'Russian World' concept

19 Pirkka Tapiola, then Senior Adviser for Ukraine, Belarus and Moldova in the Policy Unit of the EU Council Secretariat, September 2006.

20 Sergei Karaganov, 'A Revolutionary Chaos of the New World', *Russia in Global Affairs Online*, 28 December 2011, http://eng.globalaffairs.ru/pubcol/A-revolutionary-chaos-of-the-new-world-15415.

21 Mikhail Troitsky, 'Containment Must Be Overcome', *Russia in Global Affairs Online*, 25 December 2010.

22 James Sherr and Steven Main, *Russian and Ukrainian Perceptions of Events in Yugoslavia* (Camberley: Conflict Studies Research Centre, May 1999), p. 5.

23 *Energy Strategy of Russia to 2020.*

24 *Obzor vneshney politiki Rossiyskoy Federatsii* (see Chapter 3, note 47).

describe compatriots as a means to expand influence and attract investment to the 'motherland'.[25] The Ministry of Foreign Affairs' 2010 'programme' on the relationship between Russia's foreign policy and development sets out the ambition of enlisting Western business as an instrument of Russia's modernization while taking advantage of Western countries' 'declining investment interest' in the near abroad to secure Russia's control of their infrastructure and economic assets.[26] What is instrumentalized is invariably securitized. The 'Russian World' is defined, *inter alia*, as a 'transnational and transcontinental association' displaying 'loyalty' to Russian culture.[27] It is Putin's firm belief that Russia's rivals 'have tried and are trying' to 'break' this 'cultural code', which unites both ethnic Russians and those whom Russia has influenced.[28] Language, history and culture are deemed vitally important for Russia's interests in the near abroad and its own future.

Business

One of the most striking contrasts between Soviet and post-Soviet reality is Russia's growing integration into the world economy. But it is not always clear whether the process is globalizing Russian business or expanding the sway of business practices that in the main are not liberal, transparent or divorced from state and political interest. Free markets do not exist in nature. They are the products of supply and demand, and of law and institutions. In a Hobbesian world, the law of the market is no different from the law of the gun. The Russian market is less Hobbesian than it was in the 1990s, but it is harsh. To Russia's mega-economic actors, markets exist wherever money-commodity relations exist, however unbalanced, inequitable or monopolistic they are. From the perspective of liberal economists (and the European

---

25 In Putin's words, they must 'help their motherland in its constructive dialogue with foreign partners' ('Speech to the Congress of Compatriots').
26 'Draft Program for the Effective Exploitation on a Systemic Basis of Foreign Policy Factors for the Purposes of the Long-Term Development of the Russian Federation, as of 10 February 2010', MFA, excerpted in *Russian Newsweek*, 11 May 2010..
27 V Tishkov, 'Noviy i stariy "russkiy mir"' ['New and Old Russian World', cited in Pelnens (ed.), *The 'Humanitarian Dimension' of Russian Foreign Policy Toward Georgia, Moldova, Ukraine and the Baltic States*, p. 45.
28 Putin, 'The National Question'.

Commission), monopoly is the antithesis of markets, which, in principle, mean choice for buyer and seller.[29]

In five other respects, the Russian economy differs from the liberal economy. First, the distinction between state and private is fragile and amorphous. Property rights are tenuous. Roughly half the economy is in state hands, and the other half finds it difficult to remain independent of the state. (In 2009, Arkady Dvorkovich said that 'there is no legal small business in the country'.[30]) The relationship between politics, business and crime is another reality, which Dmitry Medvedev, like Boris Yeltsin, has criticized rather than addressed.[31]

Second, there has been a growing tendency towards monopolization and with it, a spiralling of costs. Elsewhere, when wealth increases, competition intensifies and prices are forced down. In Russia, monopolistic and anti-competitive practices prevent this. These anti-competitive practices include increasingly exorbitant transaction fees for bureaucrats and other intermediaries.[32]

Third, economic relations are networked rather than rules-based. Ownership structures are difficult to unravel, and networks can be ruthless when crossed.[33] Contracts have less sanctity than 'understandings', which tend to evolve in the course of implementation. Formal institutions count for little. The legal order is, for those without connections, arbitrary, and for those who have them, negotiable.

Fourth, Soviet aspirations to autarky have been abandoned, but as Andrew Wood notes, 'an instinct towards economic autonomy' persists along with a mercantilist ethos that 'encourages protectionism and a

29 Thus, with Russia clearly in mind, the European Commission decries the 'discrimination and abuse' of monopoly and the overwhelming dependence of several member states on 'a single supplier'. *Communication from the Commission to the European Council and the European Parliament: An Energy Policy for Europe* {SEC(207) 12} (Brussels 10 January, 2007 COM(2007) 1 final). [Hereafter, *Communication*]

30 Arkady Dvorkovich (then Assistant to President Medvedev), Valdai Club lunch, 12 September 2009.

31 On Yeltsin, see Sherr, 'Russia: Geopolitics and Crime'. See also Dmitry Medvedev, 'Poslaniye Prezidenta Federal'nomu Sobraniyu' ['President's Address to the Federal Assembly'], 30 November 2010.

32 Vladislav Inozemtsev, REP Roundtable Summary, 'The Resource Curse and Russia's Economic Crisis', 10 March 2009, pp. 2ff.

33 For a painstakingly researched, but by no means definitive roadmap of these interests, see. Nikolay Petrov, *Rossia-2010: Men'she stabil'nosti, bol'she publichnoy politiki* [*Russia 2010: Less Stability, More Public Politics*], Moscow Carnegie Centre Briefing, Vol. 3, March 2011.

belief in zones of special interests'.[34]

And, fifth, 'special service' professionals play a facilitating and enabling role in leading economic entities with investments and interests abroad. The commercialization of these services has brought their methods into business and expanded their reach. In so doing it has also expanded covert networks, opaque decision-making and the view that information is a tool of 'struggle' rather than a public good.

Despite these conditions, Western businesses make big money in Russia. Financial reward has cauterized many a wound inflicted by sharp practice – so much so that Russian decision-makers see little risk in dismissing Western strictures about property rights and sanctity of contract. Even in the case of Hermitage Capital, Deputy Prime Minister Igor Sechin is convinced that William Browder 'in terms of profit ... is a happy man'.[35] Sechin has also stated that foreign investors who want security in the energy sector should partner with the state rather than private entities.

Within Russia's neighbourhood, business has a chemistry of its own. Resource dependencies and asymmetries of power create an existential connection between economic relations and national independence. As Agnia Grigas has observed, even EU membership can afford limited protection against entrenched *nomenklaturist* networks (not always ethnically Russian), weak regulatory structures, corruptible politicians and law enforcement.[36] In these field conditions, where shell companies proliferate, money is often untraceable and the real ownership of firms disguised, Russian businessmen with local knowledge have learnt how to wage a 'financial-informational struggle' with their competitors.[37] They have also learnt how to improvise, bribe and bully their way to the top. (In 2000, Lukoil's representative in Lithuania vowed it

34 Andrew Wood, *Russia's Business Diplomacy*, Chatham House Briefing Paper, REP RSP BP 2011/02, May 2011, p. 2.

35 'In connection with his name, you can discuss everything, but not the economic outcome of his work.' 'Russia's Sechin defends investment climate', *Wall Street Journal*, 22 February 2011.

36 Agnia Grigas, *Legacies, Coercion and Soft Power: Russian Influence in the Baltic States* (Chatham House Briefing Paper, REP RSP BP 2012/04, August 2012).

37 In one documented case, the privatization of Ukraine's Mykaylovskiy Aluminium Plant, there were two notionally separate Russian contenders, both in fact controlled by the same group, and two supposedly Ukrainian companies. Of these, the first was controlled by the former Russian group and the second by a rival Russian group, albeit registered in Ukraine. *SWB*, 14 March 2000.

would either acquire the Mazeikiai Nafta refinery or 'turn it into a pile of scrap metal').[38] Even the mastodons of Ukrainian heavy industry, as unyielding and turf-conscious as their Russian counterparts, can be worn down by punitive energy pricing and Russian competitors backed by interest-free loans from Vneshekonombank (VEB), which has become an arm of the state.[39] Overtly discriminatory measures, including boycotts and embargoes, round out the suite of tools.[40] As James Nixey has noted, it is not in the European parts of the former Soviet Union but in the personalized autocracies of Central Asia that these methods founder.[41]

In places friendly to Russian interests, the synergy between politics and business can be equally untransparent and worrying to others. The Russian–Venezuelan relationship is driven by geopolitics, energy and arms sales, but it would be difficult to say how profitable it is. Venezuela's enormous purchases of Russian arms since 2005 (estimated at $10 billion by Bloomberg) appear to be financed by joint energy projects, the latest of which, agreed between then President Hugo Chávez and Sechin in September 2012, is estimated to be worth $38 billion. That deal accompanies an agreement to construct a nuclear power station and research reactor, which has aroused the interest of the United States and the International Atomic Energy Agency (IAEA).

Banks play an androgynous role. VEB, funded directly by the government, is tasked with supporting the development of the Russian economy, but as noted above, it also provides interest-free loans for unfriendly Russian takeovers of businesses in Russia's near abroad. Standard & Poor's classifies it as a 'government-related entity with an almost certain likelihood of extraordinary support from the Russian government in case of financial difficulties'. The whole of VTB Group (which includes Vneshtorgbank and the once city-owned Bank of

38 Interview with US Ambassador Keith Smith, *Lietuvos Rytas*, 4 April 2000 (*SWB*, 25 April 2000).

39 In 2009 VEB acquired ownership of *Prominvestbank*, one of Ukraine's largest and also financed the acquisition of the Industrial Union of Donbass by Russian interests in 2010. James Greene, *Russia's Responses to NATO and European Union Enlargement and Outreach*, Chatham House Briefing Paper, REP RSP BP 2012/02, June 2012, fn 29.

40 Jakob Hedenskog and Robert L. Larsson, *Russian Leverage on the CIS and Baltic States* (Stockholm: Swedish Defence Research Agency (FOI), 2007), pp. 60–77.

41 James Nixey, *The Long Goodbye: Waning Russian Influence in the South Caucasus and Central Asia*, Chatham House Briefing Paper, REP RSP BP 2012/03, June 2012, pp. 8–11.

Moscow) is 75 per cent funded by the Federal Agency of State Property Management. It 'has become primarily a profit-seeking enterprise that competes with private sector banks but remains close to the government'.[42] It also has a strong international presence and is beginning to acquire a visible profile in America's so-called backyard.

Much of the truly independent business sector seeks to break the mould entirely, but independence in Russia means vulnerability. Some industries small enough to fall below the state's radar (e.g. food processing) have done well in foreign markets. For a brief period after Ukraine's Orange Revolution, a number of similarly motivated enterprises migrated, hoping for a better environment (though they were soon disappointed).

It remains to add that those who are powerful enough can 'achieve partial independence'. Leading players in the metals industry, under private ownership but closely networked with the state, learnt some time ago to play by Russian rules in Russia and international rules abroad. At home, the environmental record of GMK Norilsk Nikel is notorious; in Montana and Western Australia, it adheres to local standards. Its acquisition of Canada's LionOre Mining in 2007 (which made it the largest nickel producer in the world) was a purely commercial decision, as was its 2010 decision to sell Stillwater Mining in Montana. OK Rusal (the world's largest aluminium producer) invests in many areas of geopolitical interest to the Russian state (e.g. the Caribbean), but so far there is little to suggest that these investments are not commercially led. A further complexity lies in the fact that the intertwining of politics and business is not always a recipe for submission to the Kremlin. Close connections of the sort developed between Vladimir Potanin (chairman of Interros and largest shareholder of Norilsk Nikel), Mikhail Prokhorov (former CEO of Norilsk Nikel and presidential candidate in 2012) and Aleksandr Khloponin (former chairman of Norilsk Nikel and now presidential plenipotentiary to the North Caucasus Federal District) provide buffers and allies. More than once, the metals industry has stood up to the Kremlin and insisted that it would pursue a business-led strategy.

Nevertheless, there is much opaque matter here. In October 2012, only seven months after the chairman of Hong Kong's Commodity

42 Standard & Poor's, Research Reports, 9 November 2011 and 12 September 2012.

Exchange was elected to the position of chairman of Rusal's board,[43] the baton was passed to Matthias Warnig, managing director of Nord Stream, whose former career in the Stasi and alleged ties to Putin have been the subject of extensive commentary.[44] Only in June 2011, Warnig was elected chairman of Transneft and two months later to the board of Rosneft. What this shakeup might signify for Oleg Deripaska (Rusal's CEO and largest shareholder) and the constellation of power emerging after Putin's return to the presidency remains to be seen. These permutations bear out the comment once made to the author by a dispossessed oligarch: 'State and private enterprise are entirely separate in Russia, but they can be reconnected in a second.'

Energy

Over the past 20 years, Russia's energy policy has caused intellectual as well as political ferment. A study that focuses on geopolitics is in danger of contributing to it. Before the geopolitical complexities are discussed, it is necessary to put the subject in its wider context. While, as noted above, the first sentence of Russia's *Energy Strategy to 2020* cites the country's 'mighty energy sector' as a key determinant of geopolitical influence, it also describes it as an instrument of internal policy.[45] Some two-thirds of Russia's gas production is consumed internally at subsidized prices. The fuel and energy complex is a means of binding together a country beset by demographic and structural imbalances, obsessed with the danger of fragmentation and very conscious of China's 'peaceful rise'. Yet the complex is not only a *vertikal* but an assortment of competing entities and a distributor of rent to authorized interests. It is a group of networks as much as an instrument, and this combination has become central to the structure and sociology of power in Russia. To those who run the country, calls to abandon this model are inherently threatening. They also appear to challenge core state interests, particularly when advanced by those, like the European

43 According to Bloomberg Businessweek, *RUSAL's* January 2010 IPO on the Hong Kong Exchange had attracted stiff criticism in view of its high debt, www.businessweek.com/ap/financialnews/D9E7RK500.htm.

44 Roman Kupchinsky, 'Nord Stream, Matthias Warnig (codename "Arthur") and the Gazprom Lobby', *Eurasia Daily Monitor*, Vol. 6, Issue 114, 15 June 2009.

45 *Energy Strategy of Russia to 2020*, p. 1.

Commission, who are interested in diminishing reliance on the Russian supplier.[46]

A purely geopolitical focus also risks conflating branches of the energy sector that have their own distinctive features and dynamics. Some of these rarely feature in Western discussions about Russian energy policy. The practices of RosAtom Nuclear Energy State Corporation, the regulatory body of the nuclear complex (including nuclear weapons production) and the motor behind Russia's nuclear power contracts abroad, have occasionally aroused anxiety in the EU and the United States. Successors to the state electricity monopoly, RAO UES (broken up in 2008) maintain a dominant position in Georgia and a significant position in some other neighbouring states. RZD, the state railway monopoly, Russia's third largest company after Rosneft and Gazprom, is a major player in the transport of oil and coal and a potent political interest as well.

More surprising is a paucity of discussion about coal, which accounts for 30.3 per cent of global energy consumption and is 'the fastest growing form of energy outside renewables'.[47] Russia has the second largest coal reserves in the world; it is the fifth largest producer and third largest exporter.[48] Coal plays a significant role in Russian energy security, not least as a means of diminishing high domestic gas consumption. But it has not been a major concern in Europe thanks to the privatized (if concentrated) structure of Russia's coal industry, its reliability as a supplier and the competitive character of the market. In 2009, 30 per cent of the EU's coal imports came from Russia.[49] But the pattern is changing, as US imports to Europe rise and as demand for Russian coal grows domestically and in Asia.[50] Nevertheless, if US export patterns change, the competing demands on Russian coal might adversely affect European consumers.

46 For a fuller discussion see James Sherr, 'The Russia–EU Energy Relationship: Getting it Right', *The International Spectator*, Vol. 45, Rome, pp. 56–59.

47 *BP Statistical Review of World Energy*, June 2012 [hereafter *BP Review*], p. 5.

48 Andrew Monaghan, *Stakhanov to the Rescue? Russian Coal and the Troubled Emergence of an Energy Strategy*, Advanced Research & Assessment Group, Shrivenham, 07/34, November 2007, pp. 2, 6–11, 16–18.

49 Energy Production and Imports, Eurostat, August 2012, http://epp.eurostat.ec. europa.eu/statistics_explained/index.php/Energy_production_and_imports.

50 Russian domestic gas consumption is scheduled to drop from 68% to 50–57% and coal to increase from 25% to 38–39% by 2020, www.srk.co.uk/en/newsletter/russian-coal-industry.

It would be even more erroneous to dismiss the energy security implications of Russian oil.[51] The strategic rationale behind Russia's oil policy is at least as important as the commercial one.[52] The state is a key player, though not the only one, and after its acquisition of TNK-BP, Rosneft has become the largest energy group in the world.[53] Yet the geopolitics of oil and gas unfold in different conditions. Unlike natural gas (which travelled largely by pipeline until the growth of LNG), oil is fungible, and the market is liquid. This in itself does not deprive suppliers of influence. In notable contrast to its position ten years ago, and at enormous cost, Russia and its state pipeline monopoly, Transneft, have acquired surplus export capacity. New pipelines, such as the Baltic Pipeline System and BPS-II, diminish reliance on problematic transit countries. In bypassing Baltic ports and reducing shipments across the Druzhba pipeline, Russia also increases its leverage over Ukraine, Belarus and the Baltic states. The fact that oil is fungible does not mean that every state that is dependent on it can find alternative supplies with ease.[54] The East Siberia–Pacific Ocean pipeline (ESPO), which affords Russia greater ability to redirect oil from Europe to Asia and between Asian suppliers, is the latest enhancement of its market power. Moreover, Russian participation in international pipeline projects, such as Samsun–Ceyhan and Burgas–Alexandroupolis, has been parlayed against third-party cooperation in gas projects, notably South Stream. Finally, some have deduced an intention to replace Brent as a crude oil pricing mechanism with a Urals benchmark.[55] These projects demonstrate that there is more to energy security than preventing disruption of supply.

Despite these realities, it is Russian gas that has commanded the most attention in Europe. This attentiveness arises for four reasons. First, so long as gas is delivered by pipeline, the consumer is directly tied

51 At the end of 2011 Russia was the world's second largest producer of oil but only seventh largest in terms of reserves. *BP Review*, pp. 6, 8, bp.com/statisticalreview.

52 Adnan Vatansever, *Russia's Oil Exports: Economic Rationale Versus Strategic Gains*, Carnegie Papers, No. 116, December 2010, pp. 16–18.

53 Measured by production and proven reserves. 'Rosneft: supermajor in the making', *Financial Times*, 2 April 2013.

54 Lithuania's continued reliance on the port of Butinge after Russia cut the Lithuanian spur of Druzhba pipe in 2006 demands substantial new investment. Latvia remains 98% dependent on Russian oil imports, www.eia.gov/countries.

55 'Russia Sets European Oil Export, Benchmark Grand Plan', Platts, 18 May 2012, www.platts.com/RSSFeedDetailedNews/RSSFeed/Oil/8304540.

to the supplier. Alternatives demand alternative infrastructure. (Even LNG demands the construction of LNG terminals.) Second, before the rise of Rosneft and enhancement of the role of Transneft, gas was the energy source most closely linked to the Russian state. Unlike Rosneft, Gazprom is not only the pre-eminent gas producer; it is accorded an exclusive right to own and operate gas pipelines in Russia and is a joint operator of several external pipelines as well. Third, despite recent changes in the market, there remain serious concerns about Gazprom's ability to meet consumer demand in Russia and abroad. According to the International Energy Agency, Russia will have to replace 80 per cent of current production by 2035 at an estimated cost of $730 billion.[56] Finally, the 2005–06 and 2008–09 gas crises underscored Europe's vulnerability (if not sufficiently to overcome bottlenecks in the construction of pipeline interconnectors).

One commonality across the sector is that Russia is a high-cost producer. Oil as well as gas fields are becoming mature, and development costs of new fields are extremely high. Geography is often unfavourable. New gas fields are situated in forbidding climactic zones, new oil and coal fields are rarely co-located with infrastructure, and energy must be transported over long distances. Much existing infrastructure is old, and the cost of new pipelines (such as ESPO) continues to escalate. While Russia's 2020 Energy Strategy calls for coal to assume a larger proportion of electricity generation, existing coal-fired plants are notoriously inefficient. Before its demise in 2008, RAO UES estimated that annual investment of $10 billion would be required over the next 15 years.[57] All of these factors make the energy sector perilously dependent on high oil prices, long-term contracts at fixed prices and the preservation of oil indexation in gas. Maintaining these conditions is therefore an important objective of external policy. For a country that derives over 70 per cent of export revenues (and 50 per cent of state budget revenue) from hydrocarbons, the stakes in maintaining these arrangements are high.

The drive for control compounds the strains in the system. As Vladimir Milov has documented, concentration of ownership and the growth of the state since the 1990s have led to the weeding out of independent

56 IEA, *World Energy Outlook 2011* (Paris: International Energy Agency, 2011), p. 310.
57 Monaghan, *Stakhanov to the Rescue?*, p. 9.

actors in Russian oil and gas markets, the evisceration of competitive stimuli, stagnation of production, proliferation of rent-seeking and the subsidizing of inefficiency.[58] Alongside the subsidy of household consumption, these inefficiencies, according to Vladislav Inozemtsev, saddle Russia with aggregate gas consumption equal to that of the UK, Italy, Japan and India combined.[59] Yet for Gazprom's CEO, Alexei Miller, 'the regulation from a single centre of regimes of extraction, transport, underground storage and sales' is an unquestionable advantage to the economy and state.[60] Rather than reforming this model, the burden of Gazprom's policy has been to extend it downstream (i.e. abroad) through joint ownership of companies, pipelines and storage facilities. What Gazprom calls 'control of the value chain' is a synonym for control of the market itself. For Rosneft's CEO Igor Sechin and his long-term associate and patron, Vladimir Putin, the state is the solution, not the problem, and a stable state-managed framework should attract rather than discourage foreign investment.[61] Negative investor response to the arrest of Mikhail Khodorkovskiy, the liquidation of Yukos (to the primary benefit of Rosneft) and the disposal of its assets did not deter the leadership from tightening rules on foreign investment in 2008, enforcing these rules in an arbitrary manner and revising contracts at will.[62] Yet in the wake of the BP–Rosneft tie-up, many would say, 'that was then and this is now'. Exxon, Statoil and ENI have now signed deals to explore for oil and gas in that part of the Arctic Ocean in which Rosneft has rights.

The geopolitical environment is as complex as the energy landscape. Russia could not have been indifferent to the break-up of the USSR's integrated energy transportation systems or the leverage this subse-

58 Vladimir Milov, 'The Power of Oil and Energy Insecurity' (Moscow: Institute of Energy Policy, January 2006), pp. 1, 6–10.

59 Vladislav Inozemtsev, 'The Resource Curse and Russia's Economic Crisis', expert roundtable, Chatham House, 10 March 2009.

60 'Rasshiprovka viystupleniya Predsedatelya Pravleniya OAO <Gazprom> Alekseya Millera na vstreche s poslami stran Evropeyskogo Soiuza v rezidentsii posla Avstrii' ['Text of Gazprom CEO Alexei Miller's Address to EU Ambassadors'], 18 April 2006, Moscow, p. 1.

61 Thane Gustafson, 'Putin's Petroleum Problem', Foreign Affairs, November/December 2012, pp. 92–93.

62 C. Locatelli and S. Rossiaud, 'Russia's Gas and Oil Policy: The Emerging Organisational and Institutional Framework for Regulating Access to Hydrocarbon Resources', International Association for Energy Economics, First Quarter 2011, pp. 23–26.

quently afforded neighbours whose definition of independence (not to say 'fair prices') remains contested by Moscow. In such disputes, political and economic factors are difficult to disentangle, and culpabilities are rarely straightforward. But apprehensions legitimately arise when coercive practice, overt or implicit, is not an exceptional response, but a *modus operandi*. It is further cause for concern when energy is used as a point of pressure in disputes that are primarily about political matters, including the internal affairs of other countries. The concern naturally widens when such measures affect customers who are not party to a dispute. As the EU has become more affected by these realities, its thinking has evolved accordingly. A number of Russia's neighbours, once integral to the energy systems of the former Soviet Union and Council for Mutual Economic Assistance, are now vulnerable members of the EU's precariously incomplete internal energy market.

Until now, Russia's response to any scheme of energy security inconsistent with its own has been determined obstruction. Within the Baltic states, it has employed political and economic power as well as covert action to stymie any effort to reduce what is still a near-total dependency on Russian oil and gas. In Belarus it has fought and won a prolonged battle of attrition to wrest gas transit systems, refineries, storage and much of the distribution network away from national control. In Ukraine it is waging a similar battle. Within Eurasia, Russia has tried to block every new transport project that excludes it. The South Stream pipeline project is a means not only of diminishing Ukraine's transit volumes, but also of undermining EU Southern Corridor projects, whether or not the pipeline is actually built.[63] Other projects too seem to have been devised largely in order to derail initiatives undertaken by others.[64] Any effort designed to curb Russian monopoly and diminish dependencies is presented rhetorically, and understood emotionally, as a means of 'isolating' Russia and shutting it out of global markets.

There are a number of other features of Russian energy policy that are particularly relevant:

63 Similarly, both the Nord Stream gas pipeline and the Baltic (oil) Pipeline System (BPS-1 and BPS-2) have been designed to bypass Belarusian, Latvian and Lithuanian transit routes.

64 The most recent of these, the Baltic Nuclear Power Plant in Kaliningrad Oblast, seems designed to derail Lithuania's Visaginas NPS and, as with South Stream, some suspect it will never be built. Agnia Grigas, *Legacies, Coercion and Soft Power*, p. 15.

- *A record of cutting supply (or threatening to do so) and of using the price instrument for political reasons.* At times the linkage is disputable (e.g. the 1998 threat to cut Moldova's gas supply in the course of negotiations over Transnistria, but ostensibly over non-payment).[65] At times it is blatant (e.g. the 2007 interruption of oil and coal shipments to Estonia in response to the 'bronze monument' crisis).[66] In 1999–2000 (just after Putin assumed the *de facto* reins of power), Russia artificially prolonged a gas siphoning dispute with Ukraine until President Kuchma agreed to make political concessions unrelated to it. When Viktor Yushchenko replaced Kuchma, Russia abruptly shifted from a subsidy-and-loyalty pricing model to a threat-and-leverage model. It returned just as abruptly to the former upon Yanukovych's election in 2010, but has again switched to threat-and-leverage as political relations have worsened.[67] A 2007 Swedish study concluded that of 55 major energy 'incidents' since 1991, 36 had political or partially political underpinnings.[68]

- *A willingness to sacrifice short-term commercial considerations for longer-term geo-economic or geopolitical benefits.* It is thought that Gazprom lost $1 billion when it cut Europe's gas supply during its dispute with Ukraine in January 2009. The interruption of oil to Estonia halted 25 per cent of Russian oil product exports to Europe.[69] Despite its enormous cost, South Stream's value is more likely to derive from 'insurance against future bargaining from Ukraine [than] insurance against transit interruptions and/or value as a demand-driven project'.[70]

- *A reliance on untransparent and unconventional means of conducting business.* Shreyderizatsia ('Schroederization') has become a generic term for personal understandings between Moscow and foreign political leaders that elude due process and timely disclosure. Reflecting the importance of these factors, a leading Russian political scientist

---

65 Hedenskog and Larsson, *Russian Leverage on the CIS and Baltic States*, p. 47.

66 S. Wagstyl and G. Parker, 'Russia rail move to hit Estonian supply line', *Financial Times*, 3 May 2007.

67 On these two models, see James Sherr, *Russia and the West: A Reassessment*, The Shrivenham Papers, No. 6, Defence Academy of the United Kingdom, January 2008, pp. 21–23. On Yanukovych, James Sherr, *The Mortgaging of Ukraine's Independence*, Chatham House Briefing Paper REP BP 2010/01, August 2010, pp. 6–10.

68 Hedenskog and Larsson, *Russian Leverage on the CIS and Baltic States*, pp. 46–49.

69 John Lough, *Russia's Energy Diplomacy*, Chatham House Briefing Paper REP RSP BP 2011/01, p. 9.

70 Chi-Kong Chyong, 'Economics of the South Stream Pipeline in the Context of Russian-Ukrainian Gas Bargaining'. www.usaee.org/usaee2011/best/chyong.pdf.

placed then Italian Prime Minister Silvio Berlusconi in the 'first circle' of Putin's elite allies.[71] Individuals with intelligence connections are earmarked for work in domains where money and influence can be concealed, where connections with regulators matter more than observance of rules and where (as in most ex-communist countries) nearly everyone over a certain age has something to hide that Russian *kompromat* can expose. Shell companies perform tasks analogous to the *Cheka's* trading houses in the 1920s, disguising financial flows, ownership structures and the identity and purpose of entities providing products and services in foreign energy markets. In his magisterial study, *Gazprom's European Web*, the late Roman Kupchinsky warned that 'the lack of transparency, the practice of hiding the names of beneficiaries, the use of off-shore nameplate companies and the secretive nature of Gazprom's contracts with its clients all bode ill for the EU'.[72]

This review demonstrates that Russia's energy relationships have been built on partnerships of outlook as well as partnerships of interest. Not all of Europe's wealth derives from competition, transparency and 'best practice'. What Kupchinsky calls Gazprom's European web is not based on these principles. For the most part, it is a network of normal businesses and customers. But it is also a network of accomplices that in post-communist Europe has sustained circles of influence that are collusive, resourceful and opaque – and which without Russia's support, might well have withered away.

Before the two Russia–Ukraine gas crises and the 2008 financial crisis, many of Gazprom's European customers were willing to tolerate such practices and the constraints of long-term contracts as the price of stability. But, as John Lough observes, the collapse of oil prices from $147 to $45 a barrel between July and December 2008, the emergence of unconventional gas not dependent on pipeline routes, the entry of new suppliers and the progressive introduction of energy-saving measures in the context of prolonged recession are altering these calculations to the consumer's advantage.

---

71 Nikolay Petrov, *Rossia-2010: Men'she stabil'nosti, bol'she publichnoy politiki* [*Russia 2010: Less Stability, More Public Politics*], Moscow Carnegie Centre Briefing, Vol. 3, March 2011. An insert in the briefing illustrates three elite models by B. Pribylovskiy, E. Minchenko and the author.

72 Roman Kupchinsky, *Gazprom's European Web* (Jamestown Foundation, February 2009), p. 2. For more recent examples, see Lough, *Russia's Energy Diplomacy*, pp. 13–14.

The crisis swiftly decapitalized a large part of Russia's energy sector. In May 2008, the value of Gazprom was $365 billion; after two years of recovery, it stood at $120 billion in December 2012. Between 2003 and 2010, Russia's share of EU gas imports declined from 45.1 per cent to 31.8 per cent, and in the same period Qatar's share rose from 1.0 to 8.6 per cent. Between 2010 and 2011, EU natural gas consumption fell 10.5 per cent.[73] Imports by Russian's second largest customer, Ukraine, declined from 45 bcm in 2011 to 33 bcm in 2012.[74] The unconventional gas revolution in the United States and Canada has had a major impact on EU energy markets and may continue to do so whether or not EU sources of shale gas are developed. The swift decline in US gas prices (now one-quarter of Russia's oil-indexed export price) is responsible for a dramatic rise in coal imports to Europe (up 49 per cent in first quarter 2012). It is too early to say whether this trend will continue or whether rising demand for gas in Asia will limit the European market's attractiveness and restore leverage to Russia. Nevertheless, by 2011 several of Gazprom's contracts had ceased to be tenable, and even well-established partners such as E.oN used EU regulations to force revision.[75]

Those regulations have heightened Russia's worries. The EU's Third Energy Package, which came into effect in 2011, is its most ambitious effort to impose EU market rules on external energy suppliers, and it is backed by an extremely effective system of enforcement. On 4 September 2012, the EU opened antitrust actions against Gazprom in response to three of its core practices: 'destination clauses' (which restrict free movement of goods), denial of third-party access to transmission networks and unfair (oil-indexed) pricing.[76]

The question addressed in the next chapter is how Russia is responding to these realities at a time when Europe itself is beset by crisis.

---

73 Eurostat, 'Energy Production and Imports' (August 2012); 'Natural Gas Consumption Statistics' (May 2012), http://epp.eurostat.ec.europa.eu/statistics_explained/index.php/Energy_production_and_imports.

74 Vladimir Socor, 'Implications of Ukraine's Gas Imports from Europe', *Eurasia Daily Monitor*, Vol. 10, Issue 60, 1 April 2013.

75 Alan Riley, 'Commission v. Gazprom: The Antitrust Clash of the Decade?', CEPS, No. 285, 31 October, http://www.ceps.eu, p. 4ff.

76 Ibid., p. 9.

The humanitarian dimension

In the Russian perception, soft power and the cultural and 'humanitarian' dimension of policy are synonymous.[77] As Chapter 5 will show, not everybody exposed to this 'natural priority' of Russian policy would agree. As with Nye's conception of soft power, Russia's humanitarian dimension takes an institutional as well as a rhetorical form. But in contrast to Nye, the Russian state plays a key role in this institutional effort. Although concentrated in the 'near abroad', these efforts are by no means confined there. 'Russia is wherever Russians are.' Alongside this premise, there is another: while Russia is a 'unique civilization', civilization as such is incomplete without it.[78]

Russkiy Mir – Russian World

The *Russkiy Mir* (Russian World) Foundation, a joint project of the Ministry of Foreign Affairs and Ministry of Education, headed by Vyacheslav Nikonov, was set up by a decree of President Putin in 2007. Its founding principle is that serious steps need to be taken to both preserve and promote Russian language and culture in today's world.[79] Yet its work is as borderless as the 'Russian World' itself. As Putin explains, 'since olden times the concept [of *Russikiy Mir*] has exceeded Russia's geographic boundaries and even the boundary of the Russian ethnos'.[80] The federal law on compatriots defines the term so permissively as to enable Russia to claim as its own virtually any people whose past ties them to Russia or the former USSR.[81] Thus, by conflating the ethnic Russian and Ukrainian minorities in Moldova's separatist entity of Transnistria, Moscow claims that the territory is home to a Russian majority. The fact that eight million out of some 48 million Ukrainian citizens identify themselves as ethnic Russians and 31 million as

---

77 For example, see Vladimir Frolov: 'For the first time in Russian history, Russia has chosen the appropriate instrument to impinge on processes in neighbouring countries: cultural and humanitarian cooperation, or, soft power.' 'Printsipiy myagkoy siliy' ['Principles of Soft Power'], *Vedomosti*, 8 April 2005.
78 Putin, 'The National Question'.
79 *Russkiy Mir* official website: http://www.russkiymir.ru/russkiymir/ru/fund/about.
80 Putin, Congress of Compatriots; Pelnens, *The 'Humanitarian Dimension' of Russian Foreign Policy Toward Georgia, Moldova, Ukraine and the Baltic States*, p. 47.
81 Ibid., p. 20.

native Ukrainian speakers does not inhibit Moscow from describing Ukrainians and Russians as a 'kindred' or 'single' people 'united by a common language'.[82] *Russkiy Mir's* claim that Russians 'make up the largest diaspora population the world has ever known' would appear to display similar licence.[83]

The work of *Russkiy Mir* is complemented by that of several other institutions. These include the Institute for Democracy and Cooperation, established in 2007, which has the status of an NGO. Its efforts at enhancing Russia's image are more political and state-centric than those of *Russkiy Mir*. But many of its interests – 'the relationship between state sovereignty and human rights', 'migration studies', 'extremism and xenophobia' – fall within the humanitarian dimension, as does one of its primary purposes: to 'provide Russian citizens with information' about politics and culture in Europe and the United States.[84] The institute's critical reports about human rights in Western democracies are a reminder that a good portion of Russia's image building is aimed at the Russian people themselves.

Of more direct bearing on the humanitarian dimension is the President's Commission to Prevent Falsification of History, established in 2009 and comprising 28 officials from the President's Administration, the FSB, SVR and Ministry of Foreign Affairs, *inter alia*. By what standard is 'falsification' being alleged? The Soviet rewriting of history was so notorious that the USSR acquired the reputation of being the only country in the world whose past was unpredictable. Yet it does not appear to be these falsifications of history that Medvedev calls 'harsh, depraved and aggressive', but the post-Soviet 'rewriting' of them.[85] Only following the Smolensk air tragedy of April 2010 did Moscow and Poland appoint a joint commission of scholars to revisit difficult episodes from this much contested past. Towards Ukrainian and Baltic

---

82 Both sets of figures are from Ukraine's 2001 census. Alexander Bogomolov and Oleksandr Lytvynenko, *A Ghost in the Mirror: Russian Soft Power in Ukraine*, Chatham House Briefing Paper, REP RSP BP 2012/01, January 2012, p. 10.

83 All *Russkiy Mir* citations from www.russkiymir.ru. The website goes on to cite Putin's 2007 Address to the Federal Assembly: 'The Russian language not only preserves an entire layer of truly global achievements but is also the living space for the many millions of people in the Russian speaking world.' The website *Russkiy Arhipelag* [Russian Archipelago] claims that there are 300 million Russian speakers worldwide.

84 Institute for Democracy and Cooperation, www.indemco.org, www.idc-europe.org.

85 'Russia Sets Up Commission to Prevent Falsification of History', *RIA-Novosti*, 19 May 2009, http://en.rian.ru/russia/20090519/155041940.html.

re-evaluations of this history, the response has not been scholarly discussion but invective and pressure.[86]

The Russian Orthodox Church

Patriarch Kirill I of Moscow has made himself a linchpin of the Russian World project. He has also become a political figure, albeit with the blessing of political leaders to whom he remains subservient. In 2012, *Nezavisimaya Gazeta* ranked him sixth in its annual rating of Russia's 100 leading *political* figures.[87] Religion is once again a major factor of solidarity in Russia, where two-thirds of the population now identify themselves as Russian Orthodox believers, compared with less than one-half in the mid-1990s. Kirill, Putin and Medvedev would also like to make religion a major factor abroad. In Thomas de Waal's view, 'the Moscow patriarch is probably the most effective instrument of Russian soft power in the "near abroad"'.[88] In the view of Alexander Bogomolov and Oleksandr Lytvynenko, Kirill, along with the movement's secularists, would like to transform the Russian World into 'a modern analogue of the Holy Roman Empire'.[89] At times, Kirill's role is purely spiritual, but at others it is not. In 2009, Kirill argued:

> Individually, even the largest countries of the Russian World would not be able to safeguard their spiritual, cultural and civilizational interests in the globalized world. I am confident that only a consolidated Russian World could become a powerful subject in global international politics, stronger than all political alliances.[90]

At times Kirill's role is conciliatory, but at others it is not. Towards the Georgian patriarch, Ilia II, he has been elaborately cordial and has largely kept the Church out of the Abkhazia and South Ossetia controversy.

86 M. Malksoo, 'Liminality and Contested Europeanness: Conflicting Memory Politics in the Baltic States', in E. Berg and P. Ehin (eds), *Identity and Foreign Policy: Baltic-Russian Relations and European Integration* (Farnham: Ashgate), pp. 65–83; T. Kuzio, 'History, Memory and Nation-building in the Post-Soviet Colonial Space', *Nationality Papers*, 30(2), 2002, pp. 241–64.

87 'Sto vedushchikh politikov v Rossii v yanvarye 2012 goda' ['The 100 Leading Politicians of Russia in January 2012'], *Nezavisimaya Gazeta*, 1 February 2012.

88 Thomas de Waal, 'Spring for the Patriarchs', *The National Interest*, 27 January 2011.

89 Bogomolov and Lytvynenko, *A Ghost in the Mirror*, p. 12.

90 Ibid., p. 12; Patriarch Kirill I, 'Speech at the opening of the Third Assembly of the Russian World', 3 November 2009, http://www.patriarchia.ru/db/text/928446.html.

But in Ukraine, where there are three Orthodox denominations, he has waged a relentless struggle to crush the Kyiv Patriarchate and bring the Ukrainian branch of the Moscow Patriarchate back into line.

By conflating religious belief, 'loyalty to Russian culture' and the Russian state, the ideologists of *Russkiy Mir* hope to strengthen the state's authority over compatriots and the influence of Russian compatriots in their host countries. These can be potent connections, but as the following chapter shows, they can also be fragile ones.

High culture, mass culture and mass media

Russian high culture is on a par with any other in the world. It is also Russia's purest soft power asset. The state's sponsorship of culture has paid handsome dividends abroad. But the political influence it derives from this fact is debatable. What is not debatable is the failure of many of Russia's neighbours to promote their comparatively more modest 'cultural resources'. Through the performing arts, exhibitions, literature and film, Russia delivers the message that the 'distinction between Russia and the West damages the West'.[91] To audiences in the former USSR, Russian dominance of the arts delivers a message of cultural and political dominance.

In Russia as in other domains, film has become a medium that bridges gaps between high and mass culture. The staple products of the Russian film industry are as devoid of cultural value as anything produced abroad. But the best of the rest have an indelible impact. They portray as many Russias as there are temperaments and, more often than not, uncut images of an unscrupulous world. But they also portray a culture of imperishable strength and integrity.

The products of Russian cinema provide a bridge into television, which, along with the Russian language itself, is possibly Russia's most potent form of soft power in Russian-speaking regions of the newly independent states. Apart from the obligatory quota of tawdry entertainments familiar to any Western audience, the brew is strongly seasoned with nostalgic films about an idealized or invented past, dramas about police and secret services, and documentaries about the menaced but indestructible heritage of Russian culture. Televi-

---

91 A key theme of the handsomely illustrated magazine, *Russians*, which appeared (and then disappeared) earlier in this century.

sion news is adult in tone, political in focus, concrete, informative and biased. Bogomolov and Lytvynenko are surely right to call this information space a 'hermetic, virtual world ... that effectively blocks public communication on a set of important policy areas'.[92] The question explored in the next chapter is how long it can remain insulated from alternatives.

This chapter has attempted to show that Russia's endowments and means of influence are considerable and that the current authorities have become practised at utilizing them for concrete benefit. But there comes a point at which practice becomes habit and habit hampers adaptation. It is time to ask whether that point has arrived.

---

92 Bogomolov and Lytvynenko, *A Ghost in the Mirror*, p. 9.

5 Opportunities Gained and Lost

'Russia will not start a war, but there will be such a struggle for peace that no stone will be left standing upon another.'[1]

The conduct of a state defines its position in the world as much as any resource it possesses or set of values it claims to uphold. So it is with Russia. Today, it describes its conduct as 'pragmatic'. Unlike the Soviet Union, Russia does not seek a 'social reordering of the world'. Unlike the United States, it does not pretend that it has a special responsibility to improve it. As Dmitry Trenin has said, 'Russia lacks an existential idea'.[2] But it does seek a 'reformatting' of relations with Europe and the United States, and its dissatisfaction with the present format is scarcely below the surface in any dispute or common endeavour.

For this reason alone, Russia's view of pragmatism is unsettling. In conventional usage, the term implies a wish to work with the grain of the international system and in concert with others. But in Russia it has become synonymous with 'the strict promotion of Russian national interests', which implies that these interests should not be adulterated for the sake of accommodation or deflected by the needs of others. In the 2000s this pragmatism was pursued in the service of a revisionist policy, but increasingly it has been mobilized in support of assets, clients and privileges that are ebbing away. As much as it did ten years ago, Russia opposes a new Cold War as well as the settlement that concluded it. It warns that the West is creating 'new dividing lines', yet it demands a right to dominate much of what it once controlled, and while its claim to a 'sphere of privileged interests' might not be based

1 Old Soviet joke about peaceful coexistence, cited in David Levy, 'Averting Armageddon', *Journal of Conflict Studies*, Vol. 2, No. 1, 1981, p. 26.
2 Presentation at experts meeting on European Neighbourhood Policy, European Commission, 23 September 2010.

upon an 'existential idea', it is advanced with existential conviction and force.

Not least vexing for others, Russia demands a right to be included and a right to stand apart. It seeks 'equality' and decision-making authority in values-based forums whose values it does not share and whose interests diverge from its own. Groucho Marx famously remarked that he would never wish to be a member of a club that would have him as a member. Stephen Blank maintains that Russia seeks membership of every club that has no wish to include it.[3] It also seeks to extend the UN Security Council formula to every multilateral forum where its interests could be challenged. Over a number of issues – Iran, Syria, missile defence – the message seems to be 'you can achieve nothing without Russia, and you will achieve nothing with it'. Is Tomas Gomart right to conclude that Russia 'prizes freedom of action, yet does nothing with it'?[4] How has Russia's policy advanced this goal or (if Gomart is mistaken) others?

The question might be considered with reference to the three levels of activity familiar to Russian military scientists: the strategic, the operational and the tactical. Whereas strategy governs the plans, means and 'directions' (priorities) developed for achieving overarching objectives, 'operational art' combines 'arms' (resources) and methods required to achieve intermediate goals with strategic importance. Tactics refers to the strict or resourceful employment of forces (capacities) and 'drills' (techniques and methods) utilized to achieve objectives of limited importance – but it can also refer to the primary tools and methods utilized to achieve goals on any scale.[5] To illustrate these dimensions in terms relevant to this study, both the Nord Stream and South Stream pipelines are operational-level projects in pursuit of a strategic objective: entrenching Russia's positions in European energy markets. The steps along the way (gaining Turkey's cooperation, overcoming Scandi-

3 Stephen Blank, 'Russia and Latin America: Motives and Consequences', Challenges to Security in the Hemisphere Task Force paper, University of Miami, 13 April 2010, https://umshare.miami.edu/web/wda/hemisphericpolicy/Blank_miamirussia_04-13-10.pdf, p. 5.

4 Thomas Gomart, 'Politique étrangère russe: l'étrange inconstance', Politique étrangère, Vol. 1, 2006, pp. 25–36.

5 For a comprehensive discussion of these military concepts, see Christopher Donnelly, Red Banner: The Soviet Military System in Peace and War (London: Jane's, 1988), pp. 218–23.

navian opposition, keeping Bulgaria, Greece and Romania in play) fall within the realm of tactics. So do the methods utilized: joint ventures, intelligence, influence operations, bribery, lobbying, disinformation and threats.

In no state, not even Stalin's, will foreign policy observe these distinctions with military rigour. But that does not disqualify the framework as a tool of analysis. States that fail to connect means and ends or allow immediate (tactical) goals to compromise wider (operational and strategic) interests lack either strategic competence or strategic purpose. The same is true for states that fail to enlist the support of 'forces' – people and institutions – inside or outside the country, whose cooperation is required. Pluralistic democracies are not inherently less capable in these respects than political orders organized on the command principle. As Nye reminds us in his analysis of soft power, command can be less effective at mobilizing people than conviction or persuasion. As Leon Aron has noted in his critique of the Putin system, the checks, balances and 'shock absorbers' of pluralist states limit not only power but error – though, as we know from the wars in Iraq and Afghanistan, zones of deafness can also be found in liberal democracies.[6] Those examples – not to say the wars in Chechnya, Georgia and Kosovo – are also a reminder that the relationship between war and policy remains important in the post-Cold War world. The need for a strategic approach does not diminish when we assess tools of policy other than war: energy, investment, 'support for compatriots' or conventional diplomacy. Nor does it diminish when the goal is cooperation, partnership, internal modernization or profit. Does Russia have a strategic approach or, for that matter, a strategy?

A strategic actor?

In the absence of a capable authority and an aim, strategy is an impossibility. A strategic audit must begin by identifying both. The first task is not always possible. Warlord states and failed states are not fit subjects for a strategic audit. Russia is a fit subject. At the conclusion of Chapter 1, 'Russia' for the purpose of this study was defined as the people who hold power in Russia. For most of the period under review,

6 Leon Aron, 'The Vagaries of the Presidential Succession', *Russian Outlook*, *AEI Online*, 1 May 2007.

power has been synonymous with the state. But there have been times when that certainty had to be suspended, notably during the years when Boris Yeltsin vied with Mikhail Gorbachev for authority and Soviet power disintegrated.[7] In the 1990s, the state's authority was imperfect and contested. The state was at odds with itself and obliged to share power with 'shadow structures', some of which had transnational interests and influence. At times the Russian Federation behaved as a unitary rational actor abroad. At times it did not. It was Vladimir Putin who completed Yeltsin's promise of 'reconstituting Russian statehood'. Twelve years after his accession to power, the *vertikal* may be corroding internally, but Russia remains a capable and remarkably purposeful state in foreign policy terms, if less unitary than, say, China, and this purposefulness constitutes a strategic asset. It is also, in the terminology of Maurice Pearton, a 'knowledgeable state', one that understands the means at its disposal and their potential.[8] Today Russia can be called a strategic actor.

But does it have a strategic aim? We have already identified aims that are strategic in character ('equality' in Europe, predominance in the former USSR), but so far we have not identified an overarching aim that subsumes them. Not every country has such an aim or feels compelled to adopt one. But Russia is not (in Trotsky's words) 'a country like any other'. It is a country (in Kozyrev's words) 'doomed to be a Great Power' on the basis of a 'cultural code' that (in Putin's words) is both 'unique' and 'under attack'.

It is scarcely irrelevant that Russia's most significant 'other', the United States, declares an overarching aim: the maintenance of an international order hospitable to the values of liberal democracy.[9] The Marshall Plan, the flourishing of democracy in Germany and Japan after the Second World War – and in Central Europe after the Cold War

---

7 GKChP (*Gosudarstvenniy komitet po chrezvychaynomu polozheniyu*) [State Committee for the State of Emergency].

8 Maurice Pearton, *The Knowledgeable State: Diplomacy, War and Technology since 1830* (London: Burnett Books, 1982).

9 See, for example, US Department of State Mission Statement, November 2012: 'Advance freedom for the benefit of the American people and the international community by helping to build and sustain a more democratic, secure, and prosperous world composed of well-governed states that respond to the needs of their people, reduce widespread poverty, and act responsibly within the international system.' http://www.state.gov/s/d/rm/index.htm#mission.

– serve as legitimation and encouragement to those who believe that these principles can flourish elsewhere. Yet that aim has never been uncontested inside the United States. The tensions between an idealized international order and a far from ideal world, between principle and power and between aspiration and necessity, have produced 'realism' as well as liberal internationalism. Those tensions also set limits on what internationalism and realism mean in practice, and they have established much common ground between these supposedly opposite poles of thinking. Many American liberals accept that some noble battles cannot be fought (Syria). Most American realists accept that an international order *inhospitable* to liberal democracy would pose dangers to the United States. In both minimalist and maximalist form, liberal internationalism is engrained in the American experience and character.

With similar qualifications, an overarching aim can be ascribed to Russia: *the creation of an international environment conducive to the maintenance of its system of governance at home.* This is an introverted aim befitting a country that Lilia Shevtsova has called an *odinochkaya derzhava* [solitary power]. But it has international consequences. As in the US case, the aim is not new, as Chapters 2 and 3 have shown.

That is not to say that this aim 'answers all questions', provides a blueprint of Russian policy or eliminates disagreement inside Russia's policy elite. Nor does it imply that Russia is without legitimate national interests. Almost any political authority in Moscow would regard access to global energy markets, favourable trading regimes (the EU accounting for over 55 per cent of its foreign trade), friendly neighbours, secure borders and convincing defence and deterrent forces as core national interests. The problem now, as in the Soviet past, is that 'national interest' means *regime* interest first and foremost, and any audit of Russian policy that ignores this reality is artificial. The current socio-political order constrains and skews the way these interests are defined and pursued.

NATO is presented as a 'danger' in Russia's military doctrine not simply because it is a 'military bloc' but because it is a military-civilizational force and a pole of attraction. NATO's insistence that new members adopt its liberal-democratic framework does not reassure Russia. To the contrary, it enhances its presumptive danger and its appeal to others – at the same time rehabilitating Stalin's maxim that every army exports its socio-political system with it. The geopolitical determinism of the Russian military establishment adds to the weight of this ideologically charged assessment.

The EU is not presented as a danger, but is treated as one. It lacks NATO's hard power but is an even more effective instrument of internal transformation. For this reason, Moscow invests heavily in Europe's division, in the attenuation of the enlargement impulse and in giving 'influential politicians, businessmen and opinion formers ... a stake in the current Russian regime, its policies and its development model'.[10] When Russians accuse the West of 'isolating' Russia, they mean confining this model to Russia. The more the EU's norms and practices gain adherents and traction, the more incongruous Russia's model of governance appears.

Under any development scenario between now and 2030, the EU is almost certain to require high imports of Russian hydrocarbons in order to meet its energy needs. Yet while the liberalization of Russia's energy sector would increase its efficiency, profitability and ability to generate tax revenue and investment, this course is rejected because it would diffuse power in ways that would transform the state. For this reason, Russia seeks to bind transit countries and European consumers into a malign status quo that wastes resources and constrains innovation and consumer choice.

Regime ideology defines friendly relations in Russia's 'near abroad' as 'brotherly' relations, a term synonymous with subservience. The 'dictatorship of Brussels' has also created resentment in this neighbourhood. But it has not blinded Ukraine, Moldova or Georgia to the potential of the EU and NATO to enhance their modernity and capacity. For Russia, neighbours that are corrupt and ill-governed are worthy partners as long as they acknowledge its pre-eminence. This has led more than one highly placed observer to conclude that Moscow 'prefers the weakness of its neighbours to their strength'.[11]

Russia's internal preoccupations also skew its perceptions of Western motivations. The connections between the Kosovo conflict

---

10 Greene, *Russian Responses to NATO and European Union Enlargement and Outreach*, p. 8.

11 Leonid Polyakov, Ukraine's former First Deputy Minister of Defence, *National Security and Defence*, No. 1, 2000, p. 15 (Kyiv: Ukrainian Centre for Economic and Political Studies, *aka* Razumkov Centre).

and NATO policy in Georgia, between *jihadists* in the Caucasus and Western special services,[12] and between NATO intervention in Libya and its intentions for Russia are apparent only in Moscow.[13]

The same preoccupations explain Russia's relative quiescence in the face of China's 'peaceful rise'. However unnerving its dynamic, China's civilizational model is not exportable. China has no designs on Russia or hopes for it. It is indifferent to Russia's success in Kyiv, Warsaw or Berlin. China's ascendancy in Central Asia is more tolerable to Moscow than the West's influence there. Its challenge to Western hegemony is entirely welcome, as it advances a goal that Russia cannot achieve on its own.

As in Soviet and Tsarist times, Moscow's cardinal anxiety is not that its political order is vulnerable, but that it is illegitimate. To preserve its legitimacy, it must ensure that no alternative take root on its doorstep. It must be proactive in its defence (*pace* Yeltsin: 'counter-intelligence begins abroad'). Within Russia's orbit, the patrimonial model of business must either expand or atrophy, and further afield it must secure allies, dependants and exemptions from the rules that govern others. Globally, the system requires both an architecture of multipolarity and multiple values systems and their recognition by others as principles of international order. Finally, the system of governance not only stipulates but fosters an 'image of the enemy', which simply adds to the anxieties faced.

What is noteworthy is not that these attitudes survive, but that they do so in a country whose citizens enjoy unprecedented civic and economic liberty, freedom of movement and prosperity – and in a Europe that is no longer the world outside but a source of markets, ideas, investment and a place where over a million Russians live. Russia's authorities have no wish to turn the clock back on these changes, which

12 After the Beslan tragedy of September 2004, Putin hinted at a link between the West and the terrorists: 'Some want to cut off a juicy morsel from us while others are helping them. They are helping because they believe that, as one of the world's major nuclear powers, Russia is still posing a threat to someone, and therefore this threat must be removed.' Channel One TV, 4 September 2004, from *SWB*. On 27 October 2010, the Russian Deputy Prime Minister and Presidential Plenipotentiary for the North Caucasus Federal District, Aleksandr Khloponin, warned that Western special services might aim to stir up tensions in the region in order to undermine the Sochi Olympics. Cited in Mark Smith, *Russian Domestic Chronology 2010*, UK Defence Academy, p. 245.

13 Dmitry Medvedev, cited in *Moscow Times*, 27 October 2011.

they welcome and distrust in equal measure. They seek both to benefit and to protect themselves from them. To these ends, it is necessary to influence people. But is Russia doing so successfully?

Strategic factors

In order to answer this question, it is necessary to consider the factors that affect Russia's ability to secure influence at a strategic level: its socio-political system, its material resources and its cultural appeal.

Politics, economy and society

The influence of a state does not necessarily depend on the appeal of its political system to other states. If it were otherwise, China and Saudi Arabia would have far less influence than they do, and Kazakhstan and Azerbaijan would be far less effective at protecting their interests than they are. Yet when a state is the sponsor of integration projects, and when it holds itself up as a model or as a convincing alternative to one, then it must be attractive. Russia's political order therefore has a material bearing on its strategic objectives. It is indicative that the conclusions of a recent Chatham House report,[14] in this regard at least, are consistent with those reached by Russia's establishmentarian Council on Foreign and Defence Policy. According to the latter:

> There is a growing feeling of anxiety, ill-being and insecurity in society … and of the omnipotence of the bureaucratic elite, which is estranged from its citizens. … There is no respect for law and property rights. Paternalistic attitudes are still strong in the country. Political morality has been declining rapidly, and the principles of meritocracy are not being observed.[15]

Yet what matters is the perspective of the beholder. Seen from the perspective of Washington, London and the Moscow and St Petersburg middle classes, Russia is a country with profound structural problems. From the perspective of some post-Soviet, not to say developing

14 Philip Hanson, James Nixey, Lilia Shevtsova and Andrew Wood, *Putin Again: Implications for Russia and the West* (London: Chatham House, February 2012).

15 *Russia Should Not Miss its Chance* (Moscow: Council on Foreign and Defense Policy, November 2011), pp. 11–12.

countries, notoriously ill-governed and bereft of many rights and opportunities, it is a well-ordered state in which (as the authors of both preceding reports acknowledge) prosperity has reached unprecedented levels and growth rates remain impressive, even relative to the pre-crisis EU average.[16] The country remains a net recipient of migrants, and the Eurasian Customs Union is set to increase this trend.[17] To much of the world, Russia's recent travails have the appearance of growing pains rather than inherent failings.

Moreover, these images are often coloured by resentment of Western hegemony and the perception that the reformist medicine prescribed by Washington and Brussels imposes short-term sacrifice for the sake of a long-term reward that never arrives. The perception that Russia has achieved success as a 'sovereign democracy' with a model of its own is a wish as much as a thought, comfortably stoked by Russia's rhetoric about multipolarity and its dominance of much of the post-Soviet information space.

Even before the eurozone crisis, the Western consensus had also produced an inventory of discontents in post-communist Europe. Many purveyors of this consensus conspicuously failed to ask what effect their advice would have in societies whose elites remained intact, but whose authority structures had collapsed. Fairly or other-wise, Washington was blamed for the Darwinian excesses of oligarchic capitalism in 1990s Russia. In parts of Central and Southeastern Europe, Western-inspired economic reforms, human rights agendas and anti-corruption campaigns produced similar incongruities and resentments. In three illuminating essays written between 2002 and 2004, Ivan Krastev argues that these failings reflect a systemic misunderstanding of post-communist society by the liberal West, not least the beliefs that reform 'has nothing to do with cultures' and that 'prosperity [can] be achieved simply by adopting the right policies'.[18] In her 1998 study,

---

16 In Philip Hanson's assessment, '[t]he economic difficulties facing the Russian people are less acute than those that face the European Union and the United States today. It would be quite misleading to say that the Russian economy is in decline or doomed to decline'. *Putin Again*, p. 20. In 2002, 16.7% were earning less than half the minimum wage; in 2012 the figure was 3.7%. Johann C. Fuhrmann, *Demographic Crisis: Russia's Migration Debate*, KAS International Reports, 1/2012, p. 107.

17 Ibid., pp. 101, 106.

18 Ivan Krastev, *Shifting Obsessions: Three Essays on the Politics of Anticorruption* (New York: Central European University Press, 2004), pp. 30–31.

Russia's Economy of Favours, Alena Ledeneva adopts a similar critique.[19] The argument is not that there are no good or bad policies, but that the critical variables determining success are local knowledge and the values system of the recipient. All of these failings were grist to the mill of what Thomas Ambrosio and Thomas Carothers have each described as Russia's authoritarian backlash against democracy.[20]

Despite these failings, the Western model has transformed the landscape of Central and Southeastern Europe. It is equally true, if less obvious (as Pekka Sutela has argued) that some of the initial success of the Putin model derived from Western-inspired reforms that produced visible returns only after Yeltsin left office.[21] The more salient point is that no purely indigenous model of reform has overcome the imbalances and deformities of the economies that Russia and other postcommunist states inherited. Where this did occur, some variant of the Western consensus was employed by people who understood its ethos as well as its rules and knew how to adapt 'best practice' to local conditions.

Thus while the eurozone crisis has been a windfall to Russia in psychological terms, its geopolitical dividends have been modest. Russia provided a €2.5 billion loan to Cyprus in 2011 – in the event, not enough to ward off a greater economic crisis or prize it from the EU's conditionality and leverage.[22] No one imagines that it can rescue Greece. In Hungary, Romania and Greece itself, the crisis has spawned nativist and nationalist defiance of the orthodoxies of Brussels and Berlin, but it has given Russia few opportunities to exploit. Even Serbia's nationalist government has shored up the country's commitment to the EU accession process. Paradoxically, Russia's biggest gains in Europe were secured with the cooperation of German Chancellor Gerhard Schröder at a time when Europe was at the peak of its prosperity. Since the crisis began, EU policy towards Russia has become tougher. In the Cyprus

---

19 Alena Ledeneva, *Russia's Economy of Favours: Blat, Networking and Informal Exchanges* (Cambridge University Press, 1998).
20 Thomas Ambrosio, *Authoritarian Backlash: Russian Resistance to Democratization in the Former Soviet Union* (Farnham: Ashgate, 2009), p. 1; Thomas Carothers, 'The Backlash Against Democracy Promotion', *Foreign Affairs*, Vol. 85, No. 2, March–April 2006.
21 Pekka Sutela, 'How Strong is Russia's Economic Foundation?', Policy Brief (London: Centre for European Reform, October 2009), pp. 3–4.
22 James Sherr, 'Gas Power Politics', *The World Today*, October–November 2012), p. 20.

banking crisis, it has been accused of showing a complete disregard of Russian interests.[23] Although Schröder's successor, Angela Merkel, is battling for the euro's survival and her own, she has not opposed the Third Energy Package, and Germany's energy companies can no longer be expected to toe Gazprom's line in Europe.[24]

The problem today is that Russia no longer impresses many of those whom it wants to impress. Its 1.5 million emigrants residing in the West are skilled; most of its 9.5 million immigrants (12.5 million according to the World Bank) are not.[25] Demographic trends are only slightly better than they were in 2009 but worse than in 2002. Although Russia's GDP per capita is slightly larger than Brazil's, its male life expectancy is 60 compared with the latter's 69.[26] Over the course of Putin's tenure, state capitalism has been transformed into predatory capitalism. The fusion between money and power subverts not only the activity of the state but its purpose. It makes capital, property and foreign investment insecure. It stifles incentives for innovation and renders honest competition moot. It preserves grotesque levels of energy inefficiency. It poaches resources desperately needed for education, infrastructure, health and the protection of citizens threatened by criminality and conflict. According to one grim assessment, Russia's new middle class is at the mercy not only of these pressures, but of 'mass immigration, ghettoization' and the 'degradation of accessible social infrastructure'.[27]

Between 2001 and 2008 Putin restored order to Russia's affairs and collective self-respect on the basis of prosperity and defiance of Western orthodoxy. That image and those accomplishments brought influence. Today those accomplishments have been warped by the predatory state, and Russia's image and influence have suffered accordingly.

23 Medvedev accused Europe of acting 'like a bull in a china shop'. 'Evrokomissariy obsuzhdaiut sud'bu Kipra v Moskve' ['Euro-commissioners Discuss the Fate of Cyprus in Moscow'], BBC Russian Service, www.bbc.co.uk/russian/business/2013/03/130321_eu_russia_moscow_talks.shtml.

24 For a fuller discussion, see Sherr, 'Gas Power Politics', pp. 18–21.

25 Fuhrmann, Demographic Crisis, p. 106.

26 CIA World Factbook, https://www.cia.gov/library/publications/the-world-factbook.

27 Mihail Remizov, 'Russkiy natsionalizm i rossiyskaya geopolitika' ['Russian Nationalism and Russian Geopolitics'], Russia in Global Affairs, 1 July 2012, www.globalaffairs.ru/number/Russkii-natcionalizm-i-rossiiskaya-geopolitika-15596.

Energy

Since Putin came to office, energy policy has exemplified Russia's capacity to act strategically. The problem with strategy is that it is not lightly altered. The transformation of global energy markets is testing Russia's capacity for adaptation. It is a country that excels at doing more of what it does best, and that includes applying a proven methodology to a novel situation. It is beginning to respond with vigour to the challenges set out in the previous chapter. But it is responding in a Russian way (which often means doing what is effective rather than optimal), and the risk to both Russia and the West is that this response could prove costly. Four directions of strategic activity are now discernible.

The first is to lock in comparative advantages and batten down hatches. This was first accomplished in Belarus, where in 2011 the Kremlin moved from war of attrition to end-game.[28] In December of that year, President Alyaksandr Lukashenka finally transferred state-owned Beltransgaz to Gazprom. In exchange, Belarus secured a gas price of $165.60 per thousand cubic metres (tcm), whereas Ukraine, which of this writing continues to resist similar pressures, pays $430.

On a second front, Southeastern Europe, Moscow has redoubled its pace to solidify commitments to the South Stream pipeline (which Bulgaria formalized in November 2012 before the full rigours of the Third Energy Package come into force). It has also exploited the eurozone crisis to harvest low-hanging fruit, though in Cyprus it is conducting a careful assessment before charging in to purchase gas and oil rights over resources that might be more meagre than advertised.[29] When Greece announced the privatization of its gas sector, three previously unknown Gazprom proxies had bids ready and waiting.[30]

Russia is also mounting a campaign, overt and covert, to block shale gas exploitation in Europe. Within the past year, Romania and Bulgaria have suspended their exploration programmes. The Bulgarian authorities have described the scale and organization of anti-shale

---

28 'Russian parliament ratifies Belarus-Russia gas pricing agreement', Belarusian Telegraph Agency, 27 December 2012, http://news.belta.by/en/news/econom?id=702548.

29 Ian Bremmer, 'Why Russia refused to bail out Cyprus', *Financial Times*, 26 March 2013.

30 Vladimir Socor, 'Gazprom and its Proxies Bidding for the Gas Sector of Greece', *Eurasia Daily Monitor*, Vol. 9, Issue 74, 13 April 2012 (Washington, DC: Jamestown Foundation).

protests as 'not Bulgarian' in character, and assessments of protests in Poland are similar.[31] Alexander Medvedev's statement that the viability of shale gas 'is not a matter of resources' does not appear to have been an idle remark.[32] Environmental movements have become high-value instruments and targets, much as peace movements were during the 1980s. In each case the West's exploitation of 'revolutionary' changes in technology threatened to undermine vital interests and nullify long-standing advantages – geostrategic in one case, geo-economic in the other. Far from denying their attempts to manipulate environmental movements and sabotage EU energy policy, some Gazprom insiders boast about them.[33]

Yet even if these efforts succeed, the consequences could prove problematic for Russia. The colossal gas subsidy granted to Belarus is as divorced from market realities as the uncompetitive rates charged to EU customers. The subsidy is borne by the Russian economy, and the bill will rise considerably if Ukraine submits to a similar arrangement. Moreover, as noted in Chapter 4, it is not certain that the blocking of shale production in Europe will offset the impact of the North American shale revolution in European markets. The discrepancy between the $10.61/mbtu paid by Germany in 2011 for imported Russian gas and the US domestic price of $4.01/mbtu is one factor now changing import patterns to Russia's disadvantage.[34] Finally, even if South Stream is built, many analysts doubt that it can be built economically, and by 2017 the gas it supplies might be even less competitive than it would be today. Perhaps the people who should be most nervous about South Stream are those who have invested in it. It will do nothing to advance Russia's primary energy needs, which are to increase gas production and efficiency. If the calculations of Gazprom and the Kremlin are wrong, South Stream could tarnish Putin's legacy in the same way that Khrushchev's Virgin Lands scheme tarnished his.[35]

---

31 Margarita Assenova, 'Bulgarian Government Withdraw Chevron's Shale Gas Permit', *Eurasia Daily Monitor*, Vol. 9, Issue 16, 24 January 2012 (Washington, DC: Jamestown Foundation).

32 Teresa Wojcik, 'German Environmentalists Paid by Gazprom', 13 April 2011; 'Gazprom Lobbyists in Europe', 5 June 2011; and 'Russian Assault on Shale', 8 December 2011, Freepl.info.

33 Confidential conversations with Gazprom consultants.

34 *BP Review*, p. 27.

35 Khrushchev tied his colours to a hugely ambitious programme of cultivating infer-

The second strategic direction is to exploit the unconventional energy revolution itself. Until it became possible to extract tight oil, the exhaustion of Russia's west Siberian fields was one of the few certainties in an uncertain business. Now the planning horizon seems open. Some analysts believe that the Bazhenov field contains reserves of 2 trillion tonnes, five times more than the Bakken field in North Dakota.[36] But this puts forecasting back in the realm of uncertainty. The volume and accessibility of Russian tight oil is not precisely known, capable rigs are in short supply, and the present tax regime does not augur well for investments on the scale required. At least there will be no environmental movement to block exploration and production. Successful exploitation of tight oil in Russia could be one of the few 'win-win' options in a dispiriting energy relationship with Europe. It would diminish Russia's oil problem to the benefit of the Russian economy and consuming countries. Yet unlike pipeline gas, it would increase choice rather than dependency elsewhere. The contrast between Putin's anti-shale message to Europe coupled with his aggressive promotion of the cause in Russia is all too reminiscent of Brezhnev's simultaneous promotion of NATO disarmament and Russian armament. Yet the West's politicians have yet to expose the cynicism in Russian policy and its parallels in the past.

The third strategic direction in Russian energy policy is Asia. The projected gas pipeline from the new Chayandinsk field to Vladivostok, whose development Putin authorized in November 2012, redeems Alexei Miller's 2006 threat to redirect gas supply from Europe to Far Eastern markets.[37] The opening of the Baykal-Kozmino extension to the East Siberian-Pacific Ocean oil pipeline (ESPO) might have even greater significance. ESPO is expected to provide Russia with 'switch supply' capacity, enabling production from western Siberian fields to be redirected to Asia. To underscore the point, Transneft chairman Nikolay Tokarev stated, '[w]e do not owe a single EU country a thing.'[38]

---

tile land in order to dramatically boost the Soviet Union's agricultural production and alleviate the food shortages plaguing the Soviet populace.

36 Guy Chazan, 'Russia gears up for shale boom', *Financial Times*, 31 March 2013.

37 Chris Noon, 'Gazprom's Miller: Don't Get In Our Way', *Forbes*, 20 April 2006, http://www.forbes.com/2006/04/20/gazprom-miller-gas-cx_cn_0420autofacescan03.html.

38 Agence France-Presse, 'Russia unveils $25 billion oil pipeline to the Pacific', *The Raw Story*, 25 December 2012, http://www.rawstory.com/rs/2012/12/25/russia-

The latest steps also add muscle to Russia's negotiating tactics in Asia, which (as in the case of South Stream) plays off rival consumers. When negotiations for a gas contract between Russia and China broke down over a price discrepancy of $100/tcm in June 2011, Russia immediately intensified talks about implementing the Korean pipeline scheme from the Sakhalin I field via North Korea. The Korean scheme has the additional merit of demolishing the US–ExxonMobil initiative to link the construction of such a pipeline (from Exxon's Sakhalin I field) to resolution of the Korean nuclear crisis.

As a recent Chatham House paper notes,

> For Russia, the idea of a North–South Korean pipeline fulfils a number of functions ... One is the political clout that Russian would gain in the region. Russia would increase its influence in the Six-Party talks ... and thereby restore some of its former status as a superpower in East Asia.[39]

Japan (where gas costs more than in Europe) is also allocated a key role in Russia's strategy.

Yet an Asian strategy remains a Rubik's cube rather than a straightforward task. Asian markets are competitive. Russia lost its monopsony status in Central Asia in 2009, and Canada and Australia are poised to enter the field in earnest.[40] Yet Russia continues to behave like a monopolist. China long ago took the measure of its negotiating tactics when Russia abruptly reneged on a nearly formalized oil pipeline project just prior to the Yukos affair. It perceives that Russia is more interested in enhancing its options than becoming a reliable supplier to the Chinese market. Today China has its own options, not least via LNG and the Central Asia–China Gas Pipeline. Russia faces a greater difficulty. East Siberia and the Russian Far East are an investor's nightmare. Infrastructure is largely derelict, often absent, as are public services and human capital. Many regional governments are not fit for purpose. The federal budget is bent out of shape by commitments to defence, security and the social sector. Energy costs are swollen by rents

---

unveils-25-billion-oil-pipeline-to-the-pacific/. Tokarev added, 'If they want to hold a normal, proper conversation, they should change their approach to such a dialogue.'

39 Keun-Wook Paik with Glada Lahn and Jens Hein, *Through the Dragon Gate? A Window of Opportunity for Northeast Asian Gas Security*, Chatham House Briefing Paper, EER BP 2012/05, December 2012, p. 8.

40 'Will America's zealous pursuit of shale gas derail Australia's energy ambitions?', *Herald Sun*, 28 December 2012.

and inflation. Chayandinsk gas is expected to cost $15/mbtu (versus $3/mbtu in the United States).

Russia's fourth strategic direction is the most enigmatic: sectoral restructuring. Gazprom is 'mighty' but not agile. Like its predecessor, the Soviet Ministry of Gas Industry, its focus is plan fulfilment and command-and-control. It regards competition as a form of chaos and feedback from subordinates as insubordinate. It thrives on the mega-project. It is deaf to low ambient market signals or any stimuli from below. Hence it largely failed to anticipate the unconventional gas revolution (which, like the micro-circuitry and IT revolutions of the 1980s, arose outside the boardroom and outside the box). Putin is not entirely blind to these failings, and for some years he has made his dissatisfaction known.

Now there are signs that he is replacing one national champion with another. Rosneft (the world's largest publicly traded oil company by output) is a more nimble mastodon than Gazprom. Its chairman, Igor Sechin, knows a good idea when he hears it, and he is not to be underestimated. But the company is more revenue-conscious than cost-conscious and acquisitive rather than innovative. After 2003, it acquired the assets of Russia's most efficient energy company, Yukos, without acquiring its efficiencies. As John Lough argues, the motivation behind Rosneft's acquisition of TNK-BP and a strategic alliance with BP itself might be efficiency as well as assets.[41] But it also reaffirms the old Russian principle reiterated by Alexei Kudrin: 'an inefficient company absorbs an efficient one'.[42] Within the past few years, Gazprom's monopoly has been further chipped away by OAO Novatek, Russia's largest independent gas producer. It is far from clear that these moves will have adverse implications for other established players, such as OAO Surgutneftegaz, which, like Novatek, has solid ties with the Kremlin.

There is nothing in these intimations of structural reform that addresses the country's core structural ill: value detraction. The extrac-

41 'BP was hugely successful in creating value at TNK-BP thanks to its disciplined approach to portfolio management and its application of world-class technology and skills. Rosneft has a patchwork of production companies that require integration in a way that was achieved after the merger of BP's and TNK's disparate assets in 2003'. John Lough, 'Rosneft replaces Gazprom as super champion', *Moscow Times*, 25 October 2012.

42 Alexei Kudrin, cited in Anders Åslund, 'How Putin is turning Russia into one big Enron', *Moscow Times*, 21 November 2012.

tion of rent at every stage of the value chain by politicians, bureaucrats and shadow structures is conservatively estimated to add 70 per cent to Gazprom's capital expenditure. The projected cost of the ESPO oil pipeline, initially estimated at $11.2 billion in 2004, has risen to $40 billion, and some believe it will reach $65 billion. In 2008, when the figure was only $14 billion, Mikhail Krutikhin of Rusenergy consultancy estimated that it would take 40 years for the project to recoup its costs.[43] This is the Dutch Disease that is blighting the Russian economy, not resource dependency as such. Indeed, 'the rent management system is key to the entire political economy', which is why Clifford Gaddy and Barry Ickes refer to it as an 'addiction'.[44]

Against this backdrop, the long term is hard to gauge. Rosneft's profile has risen, but Gazprom's responsibilities have also expanded: Chayandinsk and the construction of two new pipes for Nord Stream, on top of South Stream and Yamal. These projects might drive Gazprom to bankruptcy by default or, as Anders Åslund has speculated, by design.[45] If so, its disestablishment is more likely to reward other established players than bring new blood onto the scene. The innovations that Russia needs most – productivity-enhancing technology, intensive development of existing fields, and a competitive market – are least likely to materialize under the country's present leadership. The option that many experts dread most – prolongation of the status quo – might not be the worst. The worst might be what in laboratory conditions would be best: Gazprom's privatization. 'Real existing power' is more likely to turn that into a form of state cannibalism than a market-driven process. By comparison, the carve-up of Yukos could look like a child's tantrum.

Yet as we have noted, a more favourable outcome for Russia is possible. To understand the picture in the round, we must, in Adnan Vatansever's words, put 'politics and strategy back into the picture'.[46] EU energy policy and the West's exploitation of unconventional energy technologies have major implications for Russian strategic interests. In Russia, it is the absence of a strategic response, rather than its emergence, that

43 'ESPO Pipeline to be Russia's Costliest', RBC, 18 February 2008, http://rzd-partner.com.
44 Clifford G. Gaddy and Barry W. Ickes, 'Russia after the Global Financial Crisis', *Eurasian Geography and Economics*, Vol. 51, No. 3, 2010, p. 282.
45 Ibid.
46 Ibid., p. 16.

should provoke scepticism. Adjustment and adaptation – the natural commercial responses to such challenges – can be only part of a political and strategic response, not the core of it, let alone the aim of it. Those in leading positions – Sechin, Tokarev, Miller, Warnig (and of course Putin himself) – have a proven ability to act in strategic as well as in operational terms, bringing the 'combination of means' to bear on multi-faceted problems. The efficiency of Russia's energy sector is one of these problems, but it is not the whole story, let alone the strategic objective, which remains the power and influence of the state and the welfare of its citizens. Effectiveness [*effektivnost'*] and efficiency [*produktivnost'*] need to be distinguished in a Russian context. When the aforementioned individuals hear the term 'cost-effectiveness', they place the accent on 'effectiveness'.

In the unfolding energy perspective, Russia and the West face the same inventory of 'known unknowns'. What will be the demand for oil and gas in Asia, and how will this affect European markets? Will the LNG cargoes that arrived in Europe in recent years find more profitable destinations in Asia in coming years? How will environmental and manufacturing lobbies in the United States influence the exploitation and distribution of tight oil, shale and coal? Will exports continue to grow, or will they be sacrificed in order to keep prices at rock bottom to fuel industrial recovery at home? Will EU members fulfil their commitments to build LNG terminals and gas pipeline interconnectors or simply talk about fulfilling them? Will the environmental movement be as successful a foil to coal as it has been to nuclear power? Does nuclear power have a future in Europe? Will Rosneft and its Western partners succeed in exploiting Arctic resources, or will tomorrow's projects suffer the same fate as Shtokman? The only certainty is that Russia will not approach these uncertainties as an observer. It will be a protagonist.

Cultural soft power?

The various instruments of Russia's 'humanitarian dimension' of policy described in Chapter 4 have a common aim: to deprive its neighbours of any reason to pursue a course independent of Russia. Yet they are also designed to deprive them of any possibility of doing so. Measures that advance the former aim belong in a discussion of soft power.

Measures that advance the latter aim do not. The problem is that they are often the same measures, interlaced with harder additives. For this reason, 'soft coercion' is a better way of describing Russia's approach than soft power.

The traditional, imperial conception of what it is to be Russian, reinvigorated by Putin, is itself a potent instrument of influence. When Putin describes Russia as 'not ethnic and not an American melting pot ... [but] a multinational state, one people ... with a Russian cultural core', he is not describing an invention but a reality.[47] Yet the reality has produced strife throughout history, thanks not only to non-Russians demanding self-determination, but to ethnic Russian nationalists, who oppose Putin's cosmopolitan idea of Russia as much as Chechen separatists do. When Putin says that Russians are the sole nation within this constellation with 'state-forming' attributes, he is not describing a reality, but making a political statement. That statement, as well as Putin's overall view of Russia, is designed to have potency abroad as well as at home. Those who say that 'Ukrainian Nikolai Gogol is the greatest Russian writer' are not mouthing absurdities, but sentiments that spring from Russia's imperial experience.[48] Yet they are also expressing sentiments that challenge the political status quo. If the national question provides Russia with soft power, it also confronts newly independent states with a very tough reality.

While culture can be a source of soft power, its securitization is not. It instrumentalizes people. It transforms the supposed beneficiaries of Russia's cultural policy from ends into means. In Moldova, the compatriots policy has moved to the top of Russia's agenda whenever political discord has flared up. Whenever the Moldovan authorities ceded ground (e.g. over Transnistria), the issue receded. Over the harsh conditions confronting Russian compatriots in Central Asia in the early 1990s, Russia was publicly silent from the moment that four of the five states concerned signed the Collective Security Treaty in 1992.

This securitization also challenges a distinction well established in Russian and Ukrainian cultural discourse: between national origin (*proiskhozhdenie*) and sense of belonging (*prinadlezhnost'*). Russia's authorities have a habit of telling compatriots where they belong. In the words of the Russian Foreign Ministry, 'The Russian diaspora abroad

47 Putin, 'The National Question',
48 Karaganov, 'Lucky Russia'.

provides social and humanitarian support for the implementation of the interests of the Russian Federation in post-Soviet countries.'[49]

Does it? The presumption that 'the entire compatriot community is homogeneous' dogs Russia's policy in the near abroad.[50] So does its presumptive right to decide who speaks for it. As the editor-in-chief of *Baltiyskiy Mir* [Baltic World], a pro-Russian Estonian publication, unapologetically put it, 'Russia chooses its partners by itself, and no force or institution has the power to influence its choices.'[51] These are bitter-sweet messages to Russians abroad whose principal aspirations are to overcome social and economic discrimination and acquire citizenship of their titular states. The approach has led one Estonian observer to conclude: 'The aim of Russia's efforts to consolidate the Russian-speaking population ... is not to make them a part of Estonian society, but rather to push them outside society and lead them into confrontation with it.'[52]

Confrontation is not a form of soft power. Neither is a mode of cultural diplomacy antagonistic to majority populations in neighbouring countries, even where (as in Ukraine) this majority happens to be of Slavic ethnicity. The widely established Ukrainian view that there is no contradiction between having a Slavic and a European identity, or for that matter joining the EU and remaining on friendly terms with Russia, is an insidious threat to Moscow's entire 'humanitarian' project, whose primary purpose is to promote a 'binary Europe and a Russian sphere of influence dominated by a Eurasian value system'.[53]

In conclusion, the essence of Russia's supposed soft power is not to 'get others to want what you want', but to tell them what they want and, as Bogomolov and Lytvynenko argue, to 'locate and mobilize those who already want it'.[54] Russian cultural policy does not simply promote

49 Alexander Tschepurin, 'Orientir: kongress sootehestvennikov' ['Guide to the Congress of Compatriots'], *Mezhdunarodnaya Zhizn'*, No. 6, 2009.

50 Pelnens, *The 'Humanitarian Dimension' of Russian Foreign Policy Toward Georgia, Moldova, Ukraine and the Baltic States*, p. 62.

51 Dmitriy Kondrashov, 'Mify o sootechestvennikah i seansy ikh razoblacheniya' ['Myths about compatriots and sessions of their exposure'], *Baltiyskiy Mir* [*Baltic World*], No. 3, 2009, pp. 18–20.

52 Juhan Kivirähk, 'How to Address the "Humanitarian Dimension" of Russian Foreign Policy?' (Tallinn: International Centre for Defence Studies), 3 February 2010.

53 Greene, *Russia's Responses to NATO and European Union Enlargement and Outreach*. p. 18.

54 Bogomolov and Lytvynenko, *A Ghost in the Mirror*, p. 15.

Russian culture. It challenges the integrity and 'authenticity' of other national cultures in the former USSR and the East Slavic world. In part this is done by design (e.g. conflating Ukrainian and Russian minorities in Transnistria into a 'Russian' majority).[55] But it is also an expression of insensitivity. The common thread in declarations about Russian 'love' for Ukraine and the 'commonality' of the two peoples is an absence of any awareness of the offence that is caused.[56] Thus it is not simply the role of the state that makes Russian soft power less than soft, but the fact that in tone and character it divides rather than unites. It helps to keep neighbours weak, difficult to govern and dependent. For these reasons, it engenders even more bitterness when it succeeds than when it fails. Russia might come to rue this, and if its fortunes change in the course of time, it might lose all.

The 'operational' dimension

In a characteristically astute and provocative article, Sergey Karaganov, the Chairman of the Council of Foreign and Defence Policy, takes issue with Western criticisms of Russia as a country 'practising 19th Century diplomacy and using outdated notions and methods'.[57] One should indeed take issue with this caricature. During Putin's initial years in power, the strength of Russian 'pragmatism' lay in its flexibility. Old methods were used in the service of new aims (guaranteeing access to other countries' markets) and new methods were used in pursuit of old ones. Spheres of influence, domination of 'space', cultivation of clients and the exclusion of 'hostile' (non-Russian) military blocs from the vicinity of one's borders are classic nineteenth-century aims. Yet securing these aims by energy supply, as opposed to military dominance, by downstream assets rather than military bases, by infiltration of

---

55 A characteristically subtle example arose in the 2012 Summer Olympics in the biographies of athletes supplied to LOCOG (the London Olympics organizing committee) by its Russian analogue. Those who were born in non-Slavic parts of the former USSR had their details recorded directly. Those born in Ukraine had their birthplace recorded as 'Russia' (private communication with the author).

56 At a roundtable discussion in Kyiv in 2006 at which the author was present, Russia's ambassador Viktor Chernomyrdin pounded the table and declared that 'only Russia loves Ukraine' – at which point several Ukrainians known for their pro-Russian leanings turned red with anger.

57 Karaganov, 'Lucky Russia'.

boardrooms and environmental movements rather than trade unions and peace movements, by 'informational struggle' and lobbying structures, and by *kompromat* and intelligence methods of business is what makes Russia's policy novel and, in some domains, effective.

It also makes Russia an accomplished operational-level player. A strategist never contemplates an end without contemplating the means. A practitioner in operational art knows how to employ means in combination. The leveraging of hard and soft methods, of inducements and threats, of fears and hopes is elementary Leninist methodology. As Lenin himself put it, 'in pursuit of a revolutionary goal, any means are permissible: seduction, blackmail, knuckle dusters and boiling water'.[58] The same is true when the aim is not revolutionary, but reactionary or simply pecuniary and venal. This incongruity of means is what makes it so difficult to talk about Russian soft power, because it is usually accompanied by something harder. It is worth noting how the Soviet definition of 'active measures' has been rewritten in order to 'achieve business objectives'. This is done, as Aleksandr Doronin points out, by:

> forming a favourable public image of [a firm's] management, strengthening its authority and trust among partners and clients, developing strategic and tactical disinformation against competitors and opponents, undermining and weakening their positions in the market as well as their influence in politics.[59]

Christopher Donnelly has called this multi-dimensional and morally uncomplicated approach 'hyper-competition'. Partners, competitors and opponents who are ill-prepared for hyper-competition are at risk of being outmanoeuvred, irrespective of the wealth, power or technology at their disposal. Those who believe that the West faces a choice between 'partnership' and 'confrontation' with Russia will be outmanoeuvred systematically.

Yet understanding operational-level effectiveness and possessing it are not the same thing. To act operationally, one needs a way of turning the multiplicity of instruments into a concert. The easiest conclusion to come to is that this requires a conductor, and this is an eminently

---

58 Leon Trotsky et al., *Their Morals and Ours: The Class Foundations of Moral Practice, A Debate on Ends and Means* (New York: Pathfinder, 5th edn, 1973), pp. 48–49.

59 Aleksandr Doronin, 'Aktivniye meropriatiya: informatsionno-psikhologicheskoe vosdeiystie' [Active Measures: Informational-Psychological Influence'] from his book *Biznes-razvedka [Business Intelligence]*, reprinted in *Agentura*, August 2009.

Russian conclusion. The *vertikal* presided over by Putin was possibly felt in the 'near abroad' even before it was felt at home. Previously, when Kyiv, Tbilisi and Chisinau had problems with Russian military garrisons, businesses and energy companies, they could not be sure which part of the Russian state knew about it and whom to talk to. After Putin came to power, they knew. The innovation was not so much that the *vertikal* had been reconstructed, but that it had been done in a way that brought privatized businesses into concert with the state.

Yet this 'top down' culture produces deficiencies and deformities of its own, and that constructed under Putin is no exception. Its principal deficiency is an absence of *horizontal* integration: lateral communication and networking between institutions and individuals with overlapping responsibilities. Horizontal integration is also a requirement for operational-level effectiveness. It is this capacity, at which 'bottom up' cultures excel, that was so lacking as the outrages in Beslan and the Dubrovka theatre in Moscow unfolded. 'Divide and rule', which is endemic to the Soviet/Russian culture of power, adds distrust and intrigue to this excessively stovepiped formula, along with the view that information is a source of power rather than a public good. To extend the earlier metaphor, an orchestra of strangers will not produce fine music even under the finest conductor, whereas a well-rehearsed chamber ensemble will do so in the absence of one. The problem faced by a Putinist Russia in decline is that criminals and terrorists are better at horizontal integration than the authorities.

Russia's operational-level success is therefore limited and relative. Not only do many of its neighbours lack an effective *vertikal*, they lack effective mechanisms of horizontal integration. Belarus is an exception to the first rule (as, in aspiration at least, is Yanukovych's Ukraine), and Georgia a partial exception to the second. These countries remain resistant to Moscow's scheme of 'firm good-neighbourliness', and they have not become less attached to their own sovereignty over time.

At the operational level, the West's comparative disadvantage is less of capacity than of attitude. For most Western governments, operational-level thinking about Russia is a luxury they do not have, and for some it is a way of thinking they do not understand. One of the few exceptions, Germany, has devised an operational-level approach that is coherent and receives high priority. But until recently, it has been entirely devoid of hard elements.

Tactics or habit?

This study has identified a number of tactics that play a role in Russia's policy and conduct. Most of them have Tsarist or Leninist pedigrees, but they have been refurbished to fit the 'economization' of policy and readapted to the requirements of a less ideological and more inter-dependent world. They are:

- Exploitation of division ('divide and influence policies');
- Exploitation of vulnerability (moral, financial and political);
- Penetration (of opponents and allies);
- Co-optation ('temporary and conditional alliances', client states and societies);
- Creation of shell companies, 'shadow structures' and fronts;
- Use of 'agent of influence operations' (lobbyists, PR, consultants);
- Linguistic manipulation; and
- Informational struggle ('propaganda').

It is often asked, with marked scepticism, why such Cold War practices should survive. The better question is why they should not. Their reappearance in this century has often produced effective results and imposed few discernible penalties.

But that is only a partial answer. The rest of the answer is that they survive as a matter of habit. Habits that impose no discernible penalties remain habits. The decline of Soviet power put an end to several of them, e.g. the militarization of the economy and of the country's foreign policy, autarky and the command-administrative system of economic management. Other habits went into remission but, in that dormant and still malignant state, survived: the zero-sum approach (which evolved into a more sophisticated form of *who-whom*) and the country's 'imperial itch' (which as early as 1992 was transformed into Russia's 'responsibility' to be leader of the former USSR). Yet the tactics and habits catalogued above were not fundamentally challenged. Even Gorbachev made use of them, albeit for distinctly attractive ends. After his departure, a decade of disorientation (a 'decade of humiliation') resurrected much of what had so recently receded from view.

Since then, the revival of these tactics has produced some rewards for Russia. But there have also been penalties. 'Divide and influence policies', the fostering of dependency and the belief that 'our weakness suits Russia more than our strength' has embittered many foreigners who on cultural, religious and linguistic grounds feel an affinity with Russia. In the North Caucasus, similar tactics, more brutally applied, have succeeded in uprooting traditional authority structures that had survived the Soviet period – and in doing so have created vacuums now being filled by millenarians and fanatics determined to destroy the Russian state itself. In Europe, intelligence methods of business and the monopolistic ethos have transformed interdependence into a source of friction rather than a foundation of friendship and lasting prosperity. These are unnecessary and damaging outcomes. But they are unlikely to be seen that way until Russia's political order is replaced by one more worthy of the country's endowments and potential.

6 Conclusions

'Situated between the two great divisions of the world, between East and West, with one elbow leaning on China and the other on Germany, we should have united in our civilization the past of the entire world.'
– Pyotr Chaadaev[1]

Throughout most of its history, Russia's political order has been in a state of tension with its international surroundings. Whether under conservative, reformist or revolutionary stewardship, it has also had to serve the needs of a multinational country in which the borders between nation, state and empire have been difficult to delineate and have never been absolute. Over much of its history, Russia's political order has also been in a state of internal ferment, under pressure from those it subjugated and from those it co-opted, including its intellectual class and those whose horizons expanded from contact and commerce with the outside world. The principles of individual liberty, property rights and judicial autonomy never struck deep roots in Russia, let alone triumphed, and their brief periods of ascendancy have been tarnished by compromises with illiberal political forces and by failure. Those who opposed the established order in the name of justice, progress or 'the people' usually appealed to different values. For the most part, Russia's reformists have respected the elitist principle or rejuvenated it. Revolutionaries have either replaced one form of patrimonialism with another or paved the way for others who did.

Throughout much of its modern history, Russia has also been part of Europe, if on a decidedly ambivalent basis. It was a full participant in the eighteenth-century balance of power system and the nineteenth-century Concert of Europe, and beyond its own imperial domain it

---

1 Pyotr Chaadaev, *Polnoe sobranie sochinenii i izbrannye pis'ma* [*Complete Works and Selected Letters*], First Philosophical Letter, Vol. 1 (Moscow, 1991), p. 115.

adhered to the diplomatic conventions established by the European great powers. Even Leninism, which declared war on these conventions, had European as well as Muscovite roots, and the obsession of the early Bolsheviks with exporting the revolution stemmed from a conviction that Russia's separation from the rest of the continent was impossible. It was the failure of this project that led to the brutal truncation of relations with Europe that characterized most of the Soviet period. The lurid and draconian means employed to insulate the country from 'bourgeois contagion' testified both to the country's susceptibility to such contagion and to the residual fear among Stalin's henchmen and Brezhnev's ideologists that Russia was a part of European civilization. That isolation came to a dramatic end in 1991, but the same cannot be said for all the apprehensions that produced it – apprehensions that have deepened since the 'era of romanticism' about the West ended in the mid-1990s. The current authorities have sought to reconcile this apprehension with the openness dictated by their own geopolitical and geo-economic aspirations. Instead of Europe's exclusion, they seek European (and Western) legitimation of the political and economic order they wish to uphold in Russia and its immediate neighbourhood

The first purpose of this study has been to elucidate the connection between the Russian authorities' internal interests, their international conduct and their approach to influencing others. When Lenin described the separation of internal from foreign affairs as 'erroneous', he was speaking both as a Marxist and as a Russian. The methods and stratagems devised to link these domains in the post-Soviet era have a Leninist pedigree, and in the 'space' that lies between Europe and Russia, the 'near abroad', they also have pre-Soviet antecedents, based upon traditions of state- and empire-building that arose after the sixteenth century. These traditions took root in a fluid and unforgiving environment that provided multiple reminders of the Tartar-Mongol conquest and preserved a primordial fear that no matter what was gained, all could be lost. The power of the empire never overcame its cleavages, either national or social. No Age of Enlightenment, no faith in equilibrium, no rational accommodation between self-interest and the general interest emerged from this history. The twentieth century re-inculcated the worst lessons of this heritage on three occasions: during the seven years that spanned the First World War, the revolu-

tion, the civil war and the period of 'war Communism'; during Operation Barbarossa and the Great Patriotic War; and most recently in the
period of the Soviet Union's death throes and collapse, which reduced
European Russia to borders similar to those it occupied in 1560 and
confronted its population with a protracted period of economic
anarchy that anyone born before 1985 still recalls. A dated heritage
revalidated by modern events is a living heritage, and it would be incau-
tious to predict its demise.

A second purpose of this study has been to bring out the distinctiveness of the methods of influence that have emerged from this experience. Russian strategic culture had absorbed the fundamental principle
of 'operational art' long before it was codified in Soviet military
manuals: victory is not achieved by the army with the best weapons
or technology, but by the one best able to coordinate the forces at its
disposal. Imperial conflicts, like modern ones, relied upon means that
were multifaceted, asymmetrical, subtle and vicious. They were also
prolonged. Armistice invariably signalled a transition to other forms of
struggle and, after a 'breathing space', fresh rounds of fighting. Today as
in the past, the combination of means that Russia relies upon – blatant
and insidious, co-optive and coercive, 'humanitarian' and destructive
– causes disorientation as much as discord, and it brings an antagonistic spirit to many a cooperative enterprise. The experience of joint
ventures, strategic arms accords and energy diplomacy has persuaded
many of Russia's partners that no dispute is really settled and that
closure is impossible.

The categorization of these methods as 'legacy issues' is belied by
the experience of the 1990s, which refurbished them and honed the
operational code of those who run the Russian state and the businesses
it deems worthy of support. As I wrote at the time, '[r]arely have old
academic demarcation lines – internal v foreign, economic v political,
military v civil – been more unhelpful' as a guide to what is happening
in Russia. Instead of reaffirming the Hobbesian notion that chaos is
the negation of purposeful activity, the 1990s revived the Muscovite
principle that chaos is simply a medium to be exploited for achieving
concrete objectives. Those conditions rewarded those who had 'a
morally uncomplicated view of economic structures and their uses'.[2]
Those who did not lost out, and many lost all.

2 Sherr, 'Russia: Geopolitics and Crime'.

A third purpose has been to show that Russia's internal order remains a problem in international affairs, albeit of a decidedly less menacing kind than that presented by its Soviet predecessor. Today's differences are not doctrinal, but values-based (in the vocabulary of the West) and civilizational (in the vocabulary of Russia). They are lines of friction rather than lines of demarcation, and they are highly porous boundaries. Not even the most anti-Western chauvinist in Russia seeks to 'bury' liberal democracy in the West. Outside the Eurasian space defined as 'privileged', the Russian form of 'sovereign democracy' is not for export. It is emphatically and resentfully defensive, albeit in a proactive form.

The internal factor sets limits to what an orthodox, 'realist' approach can accomplish. That approach, which derives national interest from 'objective' factors of geography and power, arose in response to irenic approaches to international affairs. But it is ill-suited to a world at odds over deeply subjective things, in which the state is not always the key variable. Today Europe is not divided between hostile blocs but between normative systems. This is a post-realist discord. Its component parts – traditions of statecraft and governance, law and rights, security and business, integration and sovereignty, nation and state – do not feature in realist narratives about how the world works.[3] These subjective factors have a profound influence on Russia's hierarchy of preferences and threats, and they also influence that of the West. The most striking realist accommodation across this normative divide, the German–Russian relationship, has been the product of a psycho-historical complex as much as 'objective' national interest. Even this relationship has frayed as energy, business and human rights issues have become more contentious in Europe as a whole.

To be sure, there are also factors that mellow normative discord: trade flows and commercial ties, travel and immigration, cultural knowledge and social media. But the collapse of totalitarian regimes and fortified borders has also exposed real differences between nations and peoples. Today Europe is less united in its aspirations than it was in 1990. Differences in interest and outlook have expanded from the interstate to the corporate, civic and 'humanitarian' levels, and they are used as tools of business and policy. The vast Western effort to support civil society in Central and Eastern Europe has been as political in its

3 See George Friedman, *The Next Hundred Years* (New York/London: Allison & Busby, 2009).

significance as Russia's humanitarian policy, even if it is less politicized in its purpose and more transparent in its methods. From Moscow's perspective, there is no difference. It indicts the West for the 'coloured revolutions' between 2003 and 2005 – ostensibly instigated in order to damage Russia – and it insists the West and its 'agents' seek to produce a 'white revolution' in Russia itself. Moscow regards everything done in response as legitimate self-defence.

At the same time, Russia regards itself as an impeccably realist power. Outside *Russkiy Mir*, it draws a strict distinction between internal and external affairs. It views other states as wilful, self-interested entities that will, if allowed to, maximize power and exploit weakness. It puts more faith in interest than principles and in the substance rather than the spirit of agreements. In the Russian diplomatic convention, what is not agreed does not bind, and where the meaning of terms differs, Russia will only respect its own. Détente, partnership and even military alliance do not rule out competition in areas outside their terms of reference. Cooperation for its own sake makes no sense, and 'engagement' is useless activity unless it advances a goal. Personal relationships with foreign leaders are useful if they facilitate clarity and predictability. Often, they do not.

The fourth purpose of the study has been to present an enigma. Many of the tangible and intangible assets acquired by Russia in the first decade of this century are declining. Its leading position in global energy markets is being tested by the impact of revolutionary changes in energy generation eerily reminiscent of the threat that the 'revolution in military affairs' posed to Soviet military power when the 'new Cold War' was at its height. Putin's *'vertikal* of power' is buckling, and his model of 'sovereign democracy' is increasingly seen abroad and at home as the major structural impediment to the modernization that Russia seeks and that its fellow BRIC countries have embraced. Its policies in the North Caucasus have produced a 'black hole' inside Russia's borders analogous to the one Mikhail Gorbachev found in Afghanistan when he took office. Contrary to its own expectations, Russia's victory over Georgia has done nothing to restore its authority in its southern borderlands or diminish Georgia's defiance. Its policies in Ukraine have aroused fear and resistance on the part of that country's most pro-Russian government since independence.

The enigma lies in the fact that Russia's methods slow the system's decline without addressing its causes, and they delay the realization that it is taking place. Putin is not oblivious to Russia's shortcomings. But he believes that Russia's state-managed economy is better at surmounting crisis than the stalemated democracies of the EU. These deceptive appearances are reinforced by the reinvigoration of the Eurasian Customs Union, the self-inflicted infirmities of many newly independent states and the obvious but deceptive fact that whereas Russia's economy has recovered from the collapse of 2008–09, Europe's economy has not. Russia's neo-feudal system might reward mediocrity, diminish value and institutionalize theft, but that does not make it unstable. There is a logic to Inozemtsev's prognosis that 'it will not collapse, and it will not radically evolve. It will simply be.'[4]

Now as in the time of Nicholas I and Brezhnev, Russia's strength lies in prolonging the life of outmoded practices. If these practices cannot produce a positive end – a new European security treaty, a revised Energy Charter, 'equality' inside NATO, Ukrainian membership of the Eurasian Customs Union and a new Eurasian Union – then the achievement of negative ends is sufficient: vetoing further 'humanitarian interventions', foiling NATO and EU enlargement in the post-Soviet region, obstructing shale gas exploration, blocking a Transnistria settlement and keeping Ukraine out of the EU's embrace. If Russia cannot have a seat at the table, it will be the elephant in the room.

The effectiveness of this mode of statecraft and management should not be dismissed. The Soviet defence industrial complex produced high-technology weapons systems with unsophisticated machine tools and wasteful production practices. The custodians of Russia's energy sector believe, as Stalin did, that 'Russia is abundant' and that it can afford waste today for the sake of reward tomorrow. It would be as dogmatic to dismiss this proposition out of hand as it would be to endorse it. Neither should one belittle the tenacity and acumen of the country's leadership when it has a clear goal in view. 'Eurasian Union' and Eurasian energy primacy are two such goals that will not be abandoned lightly. It would be equally unwise to dismiss the strategic implications of tactical and operational developments. Were Ukraine to surrender the Gas Transit System to Gazprom or accede to the Eurasian Customs Union, or were Serbia to abandon its European course, the consequences might not be merely local or short-term. This juxtaposition between

4 Vladislav Inozemtsev, 'Neo-Feudalism Explained'.

the systemic debilities of Russia's political system and the toughness of its custodians is not cause for comfort. Russia's current leadership is neither averse to risk nor afraid of unpleasantness. It is also prone to misjudgment. How does banning US adoptions of Russian children remedy the injury that the Magnitsky Act (not to say the Magnitsky affair) inflicted on Russia's image? How do implicit threats to Europe's oil supplies (like those expressed by Transneft's chairman) diminish Europe's interest in energy diversification?[5] With Russia's leadership now reinforced by Putin's return to the presidency and the placing of hard men (Dmitry Rogozin, Igor Sechin and Sergey Shoygu) in more critical positions, these dispositions are also reinforced, and they set the stage for a tougher and less predictable game.

The forces and protagonists currently in play pose challenges for Western policy that exceed the scope of the theme addressed in this book. But any attempt to respond to Russia's less attractive methods of influence will be futile in the absence of a coherent and balanced policy towards Russia as a whole.

Such a policy will need to dispense with illusions of strategic partnership. As Barack Obama recently said of Egypt, Russia is neither ally nor enemy. It is an important and egotistical power with its own scheme of interests, and its authorities dislike much of what the West stands for. Like the West, these authorities fear a Taliban ascendancy in Afghanistan, but they do not consider a permanent NATO presence there, let alone in Central Asia, to be an acceptable price to prevent it.[6] They have agreed to provide a US base in Ulyanovsk for a *withdrawing* force, and they hope this concession will constrain US policy in other areas. They have no wish to see Iran become a nuclear-armed state and have no attachment to Syria's Bashar al-Assad, but they have even less wish to see their profits and their geopolitical strong points in the Middle East collapse. Their role in the Six-Party talks and their Far East pipeline policy is designed to preserve influence in both Koreas and constrain Chinese and American influence in the region as a whole. They have subjected one of the main architects of

5 See Chapter 5.
6 Or in the words of Russia's permanent representative in Afghanistan, 'even if the prolonged presence of US forces could be shown to benefit stability on our southern borders, I would prefer them to leave'. Blank, 'The Sacred Monster: Russia as a Foreign Policy Actor', p. 101.

the US–Russian 'reset', Ambassador Michael McFaul, to a campaign of sustained abuse and have transformed another of its architects, former Secretary of State Hillary Clinton, into an object of vilification. Putin's re-election campaign raised anti-Americanism to a level not seen since the election of Ronald Reagan. Russia's largest military exercise since the Second World War, Zapad-2009, unfolded against the background of a hypothetical NATO attack on Belarus (in defence of Polish and Lithuanian 'compatriots') and closed with a simulated nuclear strike on Warsaw. The reaction to NATO missile defence has been not just threats but also programmes to modernize Russia's theatre nuclear forces and develop low-yield nuclear weapons. The vituperative reaction of the Kremlin and the Ministry of Foreign Affairs to the conviction of the Russian arms smuggler Viktor Bout was worth a thousand declarations about fighting organized crime. Although these examples do not make Russia a 'foe' (*pace* Mitt Romney), they are not the actions of a partner.

The West will also need to abandon the conceit that Russia faces a choice between pro- and anti-Western alternatives. Russia's political figures are at best pro-Russian and at worst only interested in their own aggrandizement. A less authoritarian Russia will not necessarily be more liberal towards Russia's neighbours; a less corrupt Russia will not necessarily be more democratic. There are thoughtful and potent forces in the country that loathe corruption, demand good governance, support the rule of law and admire the ideas of French far-right leader Marine Le Pen.[7] These are not contradictory ideas in a Russian context. Neither is opposition to Putin's vision of Eurasian Union and the belief that Russia, Ukraine and Belarus should be united in a Slavic Union without Caucasian or Central Asian responsibilities and immigrants.[8] Terms like 'liberal', 'democrat' and 'nationalist' make people and choices appear far simpler than they are.

For these reasons alone, calls for Western 'moral leadership' should be distrusted. The West has its own principles and should not conceal

---

7 Mikhail Rezimov, 'Russkiy natsionalizm i rossiyskaya geopolitika: poiydet li Rossiya putem Turtsii?' ['Russian Nationalism and Russian Geopolitics: Will Russia Go the Way of Turkey?'], *Rossiya v Globalnoy Politike* [*Russia in Global Affairs*], 1 July 2012, p. 6, www.globalaffairs.ru/number/Russkii-natcionalizm-i-rossiiskaya-geopolitika-15596.

8 Paul Goble, 'Slavic Nations Don't Want Union with Central Asia, Moscow Researcher Says', *Window on Eurasia*, 17 December 2012, http://windowoneurasia2.blogspot.com/2012/12/window-on-eurasia-slavic-nations-dont.html.

them. But its experience of influencing Russia's internal affairs has hardly been the best, even when (as in the Yeltsin era) such influence took place by invitation. Paradoxically, its limited successes occurred during the Cold War rather than after it. In the 1970s, specific gains (e.g. the relaxation of policy on Jewish emigration) were secured because the Soviet authorities anticipated gains for themselves in return and because they judged their key Western interlocutor, the Nixon administration, to be predictable and serious. In the early 1980s the Reagan administration undertook a range of measures to support the system's opponents in its soft underbelly, the Socialist Commonwealth of Central Europe, and reverberations in the non-Russian republics of the USSR followed. Yet this was an overtly antagonistic and high-risk policy that arose at a time when the Cold War was at its height. It would not have succeeded without coordination at the highest level. The policy posed no discernible risk to other US interests and entailed no economic cost beyond that already imposed by the militarized East–West confrontation. As the Cold War entered its *dénouement*, human rights acquired growing prominence in Western policy. Yet Western pressure was designed to encourage, not thwart Gorbachev in his insistence that 'there is no alternative' to reform. In all of these episodes, the arbiter in Moscow's actions was Soviet political interest.

Today, the West is less united than it has been at any time since the Marshall Plan. So, too, is the opposition in Russia, a fair portion of which is as disdainful of the West as it is of the regime in Moscow it reviles. The structure of trade and investment sets sobering limits on what the West is willing to risk and able to accomplish. The impact on mindsets, budgets and bureaucracies of the West's more acute priorities needs no restatement. In these conditions, a policy of 'moral leadership' will swiftly default into rhetoric and symbolic steps, which in the absence of concerted and comprehensive measures will forfeit the respect of those they antagonize as well as those they are intended to help. None of these constraints oblige the West to grant visas or provide investment opportunities for individuals who steal property or commit outrages (such as Magnitsky's murder). But smart sanctions are sometimes smarter for being quieter. While they can work against small networks, sanctioning a political system is a more serious matter.

Finally, the West needs to abandon guilt. Its moral itch has damaged relations as much as Russia's imperial itch. But flawed assistance programmes did not produce robber capitalism in Russia, and while other policies helped revive Russia's encirclement complexes, they also provided vindication and scapegoats for changes that were already under way. The West should also be mature enough to accept that some measures that damaged its relationship with Russia were indispensable to other countries and beneficial to Europe as a whole. No sound policy operates without trade-offs and moral compromises. Double standards do not diminish the impact of standards or the convictions of those who believe in them. As Fritz Stern wrote in his magisterial study of Bismarck, 'the world is not a moral gymnasium'.[9]

The challenge for the West today is to devise policies that rebalance the rules of the game and the choices open to Russia. To these ends, it should:

- practise democracy rather than preach it;
- watch how Russia's business affects the West's business (*pace* Harold Macmillan);
- let Russia reap the consequences of its choices; and
- insist that both Russia and the West deserve better.

First, the West should not forget that values are best disseminated by practices and institutions. They are poorly transmitted by strictures and sermons. It is not appropriate for US State Department spokesmen and European commissioners to provide a running commentary about Russia's internal affairs. Those who 'urge' Russia to conduct fair elections or combat corruption should ask who in Russia is helped by such declarations. When such statements are confined to Russia alone, they arouse cynicism; when they are divorced from action, they are risible. Today, the Kremlin perceives that the West uses values as a tool of geopolitics. Its opponents perceive that the West confuses pieties with policies.

Nevertheless, there are times when values, not to say practice, demand robust public discussion. Russia is party to international conventions, and it has made general and specific commitments as a member of the OSCE and Council of Europe. Toward the OSCE in particular, it has a set of policies that would rein in the autonomy of its specialist institutions and field operations, as well as constrain the remit of its Office

---

9 Fritz Stern, *Gold and Iron: Bismarck, Bleichröder and the Building of the German Empire* (Vintage, 1979), p. vi.

for Democratic Institutions and Human Rights. As Dov Lynch has observed, the organization 'is both *the theatre* where Russia plays out many of its concerns... and *the object* of specific requests from Moscow'.[10] The West cannot afford to act as if such organizations are of secondary importance or allow their integrity to be compromised. Nor should it allow them to degenerate into anti-Russian forums. OSCE standards should apply to OSCE members without discrimination or favour.

The second principle underscores rights and jurisdictions. It affirms that even 'kindred people' are citizens of sovereign states and members of European society. It also demands vigorous measures to ensure that Russian entities in the EU and North America act in accordance with their laws and codes of conduct. Such measures should not be thought of as punitive sanctions but as effective law enforcement. The EU's Third Energy Package is an exemplar of good policy. Its full implementation will have a more profound impact on Russia than any number of Magnitsky Acts.

The third principle draws a line under Russian attempts to have it both ways. Russia has every right to oppose the 'dictatorship of Brussels'. But it cannot claim a privileged relationship with Brussels on this basis, let alone veto rights over EU or NATO policy. A Russia that opposes the interests and values of institutions defined on the basis of interests and values is entitled to a transactional relationship befitting its status and importance. But it is not entitled to more. With respect to the Eurasian Customs Union and Collective Security Treaty Organization, that is all that the EU and NATO demand, and Russia should be reminded of this. If Russia is determined to isolate itself, that is its decision. If it is determined to block agreement, the West should find prudent and constructive ways of proceeding without it.

The fourth principle enjoins the West to pay more attention to the country than to the Russian regime. Russia might not be a liberal democracy in the making, but it is not doomed to carry on in its present form, and it is it is not clear how long its current political dispensation might last. What will replace it is a matter of guesswork, but at some point it will assume a form that Western policy could shape for good or ill. To this end, the West needs to remind itself that the purpose of its policy is not to punish Russia, but to uphold interests and standards upon

10 Dov Lynch, seminar presentation at St Antony's College, Oxford University, 27 October 2008 [emphasis in original].

which Russia might look more positively tomorrow than it does today. For the same reason, the West should not only reconsider its visa policy but change it (without neglecting to make corresponding changes in Belarus, Moldova and Ukraine). Like these three countries, Russia is arguably eligible for EU membership under the Treaty of Rome (which Mediterranean Dialogue countries are not). Perhaps it is time for EU members, inside or outside the Schengen Agreement, to lose their inhibitions about discriminating in favour of Europe. Finally, the West should recall that some Russian businesses observe best practice, and many more observe good practice, and that it should not only afford them opportunity to invest and expand, but advertise the fact.

With respect to the modes of influence addressed in this study, the West needs policies that respond to Russia's core advantages: the asymmetrical approach, 'operational art' (the 'combination of means') and tenacity. At a minimum, this suggests three directions of Western activity.

Regenerating expertise about Russia in all relevant branches of government (which today must include financial regulation, environmental policy and law enforcement). Sadly, there is much amateurism in high places. Experts have no mandate to make policy. But policy-makers need to hear from them before decisions are made.

Public diplomacy. The West cannot allow Russia to conduct a monologue about Western intentions in its 'near abroad' or in Russia itself. Yet news, information and public diplomacy are inadequate in scope, under-financed and often out of kilter with local concerns and needs. The EU and NATO have a particularly poor record of making their policies comprehensible, let alone explaining the benefits that better relations would offer. It is indicative that while the British embassy in Kyiv has produced a concise Ukrainian-language brochure about the EU–Ukraine Association Agreement, the EU delegation has not.

Institutional reinforcement. In principle, national authorities are assigned most of the burden of enforcing EU norms and standards in their own jurisdictions. Yet this is an excessive burden for new member states exposed to high degrees of Russian influence, penetration and pressure. Mechanisms of consultation, coordination and support need enhancement.

The obstacles that lie between these principles and effective Western policies are considerable, but they are more intellectual than financial. Such policies will not jeopardize the West's current scheme of internal and global priorities, and they can be put in place by governments which have the will to do so. If some lack the will, that should not deter others from acting, individually or in concert.

Russia will continue to be defined by its contradictions. So will its international relationships. Russia's methods of influence have prolonged the life of the socio-political model that constitutes its biggest obstacle to lasting and beneficial influence. There is no way to know whether Russia will confront this paradox during the current decade or even the next. If it does not, its sources of power and wealth are likely to decline. The corollary to this decline could prove to be obdurate policies rather than emollient ones. What is reasonable to assume is that as time proceeds, an increasing number of Russians will ask whether the current model of development serves the national interest. Whether they extend their enquiry to the country's external policies remains to be seen. In part, the answer to that question will depend upon the West. It can do much to help Russia by helping itself. Today, much depends on whether it knows how to do so.

Select Bibliography

Ambrosio, Thomas, *Authoritarian Backlash: Russian Resistance to Democratization in the Former Soviet Union* (Farnham: Ashgate, 2009).

Anderson, M.S., *The Eastern Question 1774–1923: A Study in International Relations* (London: Macmillan, 1966).

Assenova, Margarita, 'Bulgarian Government Withdraw Chevron's Shale Gas Permit', *Eurasia Daily Monitor*, Vol. 9, Issue 16, 24 January 2012 (Washington, DC: Jamestown Foundation).

Berg, E. and Ehin, P. (eds), *Identity and Foreign Policy: Baltic–Russian Relations and European Integration* (Farnham: Ashgate, 2009).

Blank, Stephen J., 'The Sacred Monster: Russia as a Foreign Policy Actor', in Stephen J. Blank (ed.), *Perspectives on Russian Foreign Policy* (Carlisle, PA: Strategic Studies Institute, US Army War College, 2012).

Blank, Stephen J., *Towards the Failing State: The Structure of Russian Security Policy* (Camberley: Conflict Studies Research Centre, F56, November 1996).

Bogomolov, Alexander and Lytvynenko, Oleksandr, *A Ghost in the Mirror: Russian Soft Power in Ukraine*, Chatham House Briefing Paper, REP RSP BP 2012/01, January 2012.

BP Statistical Review of World Energy, June 2012.

Brzezinski, Zbigniew and Sullivan, Paige (eds), *Russia and the Commonwealth of Independent States: Documents, Data and Analysis* (Washington, DC: CSIS, 1997).

Carothers, Thomas, 'The Backlash Against Democracy Promotion', *Foreign Affairs*, Vol. 85, No. 2, March–April 2006.

Chyong, Chi-Kong, 'Economics of the South Stream Pipeline in the Context of Russian–Ukrainian Gas Bargaining', www.usaee.org/usaee2011/best/chyong.pdf.

Crow, Suzanne, 'Russia Debates its National Interests', *RFE/RL Research Report*, 10 July 1992.

Dahrendorf, Ellen and Willets, Harry (eds), *Leonard Schapiro: Russian Studies* (London: Collins Harvill, 1986).

Dallin, David, *Soviet Foreign Policy After Stalin* (London: Methuen, 1961/1975).

Dick, C.J., 'Initial Thoughts on Russia's Draft Military Doctrine', CSRC

Occasional Brief, No. 12, 14 July 1992.

Dick, C.J., 'The Military Doctrine of the Russian Federation', Occasional Brief 25 (Camberley: Conflict Studies Research Centre, RMA Sandhurst, 1993).

Dick, C.J., *Russian Views on Future War* (Camberley: Conflict Studies Research Centre, AA26, June 1993).

Dolgopolova, Natalya and Kokoshin, Andrey, 'Lessons Learned From the Destinies of Great Powers', *Kommunist*, No. 2, January 1988.

Doronin, Aleksandr, 'Aktivniye meropriatiya: informatsionno-psikhologicheskoe vosdeiystie' ['Active Measures: Informational-Psychological Influence'], from his book *Biznes-razvedka* [*Business Intelligence*], reprinted in *Agentura*, August 2009.

Dziak, John J., *Chekisty: A History of the KGB* (Lexington, MA: Lexington Books, 1988).

European Commission, *Communication from the Commission to the European Council and the European Parliament: An Energy Policy for Europe* {SEC(207) 12} (Brussels, 10 January 2007 COM(2007) 1 final).

Friedman, George, *The Next Hundred Years* (New York/London: Allison & Busby, 2009).

Frolov, Vladimir, 'Printsipiy myagkoy siliy' ['Principles of Soft Power'], *Vedomosti*, 8 April 2005.

Fuhrmann, Johann C., *Demographic Crisis: Russia's Migration Debate*, KAS International Reports, 1/2012.

Gaddy, Clifford G. and Ickes, Barry W., 'Russia after the Global Financial Crisis', *Eurasian Geography and Economics*, 2010, Vol. 51, No. 3.

Gadzhiev, K. S., *Vvedenie v geopolitiku* [*Introduction to Geopolitics*], 1994, updated and reissued in paperback in 1998 (Moscow: Logos, 1998).

Giles, Keir, *The Military Doctrine of the Russian Federation 2010* (Rome: NATO Defence Review, NATO Defence College, February 2010).

Gomart, Thomas, 'Politique étrangère russe: l'étrange inconstance', *Politique étrangère* Vol. 1, 2006.

Gorbachev, Mikhail, 'For the Sake of Preserving Human Civilization', *Novosti*, 16 February 1987.

Greene, James, *Russia's Responses to NATO and European Union Enlargement and Outreach'*, Chatham House Briefing Paper, REP RSP BP 2012/02, June 2012.

Grigas, Agnia, *Legacies, Coercion and Soft Power: Russian Influence in the Baltic States*, Chatham House Briefing Paper, REP RSP BP 2012/04, August 2012.

Gvosdev, Nikolas (ed.), *The Strange Death of Soviet Communism* (Special Issue of *The National Interest*), No. 31, Spring 1993.

Hanson, Philip, Nixey, James, Shevtsova, Lilia and Wood, Andrew, *Putin Again: Implications for Russia and the West* (London: Chatham House, February 2012).

Hedenskog, Jakob and Larsson, Robert L., *Russian Leverage on the CIS and Baltic States* (Stockholm: Swedish Defence Research Agency (FOI), 2007).

Holbraad, Carsten, *The Concert of Europe: A Study in German and British International Theory, 1815–1914* (London: Longman, 1970).

Inozemtsev, Vladislav, 'Neo-feudalism Explained', February 2011, http://postindustrial.net/2011/02/neo-feudalism-explained/.

International Energy Agency (IEA), *World Energy Outlook 2011*, Paris.

Karaganov, Sergey, 'Lucky Russia', *Russia in Global Affairs*, 29 March 2011.

Karaganov, Sergey, 'A Revolutionary Chaos of the New World', *Russia in Global Affairs Online*, 28 December 2011.

Kivirähk, Juhan, 'How to Address the "Humanitarian Dimension" of Russian Foreign Policy?' (Tallinn: International Centre for Defence Studies, 3 February 2010).

Kolstø, Pål, *An Appeal to the People: Glasnost – Aims and Means* (Oslo: Institute for Defence Studies), 1988.

Kolstø, Pål, *Russians in the Former Soviet Republics* (London: Hurst, 1995).

Kononenko, Vadim and Moshes, Arkady, *Russia as a Network State: What Works in Russia When State Institutions Do Not* (London: Palgrave, 2011).

Kosachev, Konstantin, 'Three Birds with One Stone?', *Russia in Global Affairs*, November 2010.

Kozyrev, Andrey, 'Russia: A Chance for Survival', *Foreign Affairs*, Vol. 71, No. 2, June 1992.

Krastev, Ivan, *Shifting Obsessions: Three Essays on the Politics of Anticorruption* (New York: Central European University Press, 2004).

Krivitsky, W.G., *I Was Stalin's Agent* (1939) (ed. Mark Almond) (Cambridge: Ian Faulkner, 1992).

Kryuchkov, Vladimir, *Deyatel'nost' organov gosudarstvennoy bezopastnosti na sovremennon etape* [*Activities of the Organs of State Security at the Present Stage*] (Moscow, 1988). From KGB documents released by the Gayauskas Commission (Lithuania).

Kupchinsky, Roman, *Gazprom's European Web* (Jamestown Foundation, February 2009).

Kupchinsky, Roman, 'Nord Stream, Matthias Warnig (codename "Arthur") and the Gazprom Lobby', *Eurasia Daily Monitor*, Vol. 6, Issue 114, 15 June 2009.

Kuzio, T., 'History, Memory and Nation-building in the Post-Soviet Colonial Space', *Nationality Papers*, Vol. 30, No. 2, 2002.

Latynina, Yulia, 'The Economy: New Actors, Old Legacies', in Isham, Heyward (ed.), *Reconstructing Russia: Perspectives from Within* (New York: Institute for East–West Studies, 1996).

Lavrov, Sergey, 'Sderzhivanie Rossii: Nazad v Buduschee?' ['Containing Russia: Back to the Future?'], *Rossiya v Global'noy Politike* [*Russia in Global Affairs*], 22 August 2007.

Lavrov, Sergey, 'Diplomatiya i biznes' ['Diplomacy and Business'], *Mezhdunarodnaya Zhizn'* [*International Affairs*], 6 April 2004.

Ledeneva, Alena, 'Cronies, Economic Crime and Capitalism in Putin's *Sistema*' (review article), *International Affairs*, Vol. 88, No. 1, 2012.

Ledeneva, Alena, *Russia's Economy of Favours: Blat, Networking and Informal Exchanges* (Cambridge University Press, 1998).

LeDonne, John, *The Grand Strategy of the Russian Empire, 1650–1831* (Oxford University Press, 2004).

Leggett, George, *The Cheka: Lenin's Political Police* (Oxford University Press, 1981).

Lenin, V.I., 'Vneshnyaya politika russkoy revoliutsii' ['The External Policy of the Russian Revolution'], in *Sochinenie* [*Collected Works*] (Moscow: State Publishing House of Political Literature, Institute of Marx-Engels-Lenin, 1949).

Lenin, V.I., '*Left-wing' Communism, an Infantile Disorder* (April 1920) (Moscow: Progress Publishers, 1981).

Lenin, V.I., *The State and Revolution* (1918), www.marxists.org/archive/lenin/works/1917/staterev.

Lieven, Dominic, 'Dilemmas of Empire 1850–1918. Power, Territory, Identity', *Journal of Contemporary History*, Vol. 34, Issue 2, April 1999.

Lo, Bobo, *Axis of Convenience: Moscow, Beijing and the New Geopolitics* (Washington, DC: Brookings/Chatham House, 2008).

Lough, John, *The Place of Russia's 'Near Abroad'* (Camberley: Conflict Studies Research Centre, F32, January 1993).

Lough, John, *Russia's Energy Diplomacy*, Chatham House Briefing Paper, REP RSP BP 2011/01, May 2011.

Lucas, Edward, *The New Cold War: How the Kremlin Menaces both Russia and the West* (London: Bloomsbury, 2008).

Lynch, Dov, 'Russia and the OSCE: Contours of European Security', Lecture at St Antony's College, Oxford, 27 October 2008.

Medvedev, Dmitry, 'Poslaniye Prezidentu Ukrainy Viktoru Yushchenko' ['Appeal to President of Ukraine Viktor Yushchenko'], 11 August 2009, http://www.kremlin.ru/news/5158.

Medvedev, Dmitry, 'Poslaniye Prezidenta Federal'nomu Sobraniyu' ['President's Address to the Federal Assembly'], 30 November 2010.

Medvedev, Dmitry, 'Speech at World Policy Conference', Evian, 8 October 2008, President of Russia Official Web Portal.

Medvedev, Zhores, *Gorbachev* (Oxford: Blackwell, 1987).

Mlynář, Zdeněk, *Night Frost in Prague* (London: Hurst, 1980).

Monaghan, Andrew, 'An Enemy the Gates: Russian Foreign Policy', *International Affairs*, Vol. 84, No. 4, 2008.

Monaghan, Andrew, *From Lisbon to Munich: Russian Views of NATO–Russian Relations*, Research Division, NATO Defence College, Rome, February 2011.

Monaghan, Andrew (ed.), *The Indivisibility of Security: Russia and Euro-Atlantic Security*, Research Division, NATO Defence College, Rome, December 2009.

Monaghan, Andrew, *Stakhanov to the Rescue? Russian Coal and the Troubled Emergence of an Energy Strategy* (Shrivenham: Advanced Research & Assessment Group, 07/34, November 2007).

Moshes, Arkady, 'Russia's European Policy Under Medvedev: How Sustainable is a New Compromise?', *International Affairs*, Vol. 88, No. 1, 2012.

Nicolson, Harold, *Diplomacy* (London: Oxford University Press, 1963).

Nixey, James, *The Long Goodbye: Waning Russian Influence in the South Caucasus and Central Asia*, Chatham House Briefing Paper, REP RSP BP 2012/03, June 2012.

Nowak, Andrzej, *Imperiological Studies: A Polish Perspective* (Cracow: Jagiellonian University, 2011).

Nye, Joseph S. Jr, *Soft Power: The Means to Success in World Politics* (New York: PublicAffairs, 2004).

Odom, William, 'How Far Can Soviet Reform Go?', *Problems of Communism*, November/December 1987.

Paik, Keun-Wook with Lahn, Glada and Hein, Jens, *Through the Dragon Gate? A Window of Opportunity for Northeast Asian Gas Security*, Chatham House Briefing Paper EER BP 201/05, December 2012.

Pastukhov, Vladimir, *Restavratsiya vmesto reformatsii* [*Restoration Instead of Reform*] (Moscow: OGI, 2012), p. 104.

Pearton, Maurice, *The Knowledgeable State: Diplomacy, War and Technology since 1830* (London: Burnett Books, 1982).

Pelnens, Gatis (ed.), *The 'Humanitarian Dimension' of Russian Foreign Policy Toward Georgia, Moldova, Ukraine and the Baltic States* (Riga: Centre for East European Policy Studies, Konrad Adenauer Stiftung, Soros Foundation Latvia, 2nd supplementary edn, 2010).

Petrov, Nikolay, *Rossia-2010: Men'she stabil'nosti, bol'she publichnoy politiki* [*Russia 2010: Less Stability, More Public Politics*], Moscow Carnegie Centre Briefing, Vol. 3, March 2011.

Pipes, Richard, *Russia Under the Bolshevik Regime, 1919–1924* (London: Harvill, 1994).

Plekhanov, G.V., *Socialism and the Political Struggle* (1883), http://www.marxists.og/archive/plekhanov/1883/struggle/index.htm.

Popescu, Nicu and Litra, Leonid, *Transnistria: A Bottom-up Solution* (European Council on Foreign Relations, ECFR/63, September 2012).

Potekhin, Oleksandr, 'Russian Foreign Policy Trends under President Putin', *Monitoring* (Kyiv: Centre for Peace, Conversion and Foreign Policy of Ukraine), 30 May 2000.

Primakov, Evgeniy, 'The organic link between domestic policy and foreign policy has never been as clear as it is today', *Pravda*, 10 July 1988.

Primakov, Evgeniy, 'Zapis' Press-Konferentsii Ministra Inostranniykh Del Rossii E.M. Primakova' ['Transcript of Press Conference'], 12 January 1996.

Putin, Vladimir, 'Rossiya: Natsionalniy Vopros' ['Russia: The National Question'], *Nezavisimaya Gazeta*, 23 January 2012.

Putin, Vladimir, 'A New Integration Project for Eurasia – A Future Being Born Today', *Izvestiya*, 4 October 2011. (*Johnson's Russia List*, No. 180, 6 October 2011, Item 30.)

Putin, Vladimir, 'Viystuplenie V V Putina na Kongress sooteestvennikov prozhivauyushchikh za rubezhom' ['Speech to the Congress of Compatriots Residing Abroad'], 11–12 October 2001, mosds.ru.

Putin, Vladimir, 'Russia at the Turn of the Millennium', December 1999, www.government.gov.ru/english/statVP_engl_1.html.

Remizov, Mikhail, 'Russkiy natsionalizm i rossiyskaya geopolitika' ['Russian Nationalism and Russian Geopolitics'], *Russia in Global Affairs*, 1 July 2012, www.globalaffairs.ru/number/Russkii-natcionalizm-i-rossiiskaya-geopolitika-15596.

Riley, Alan, 'Commission v. Gazprom: The Antitrust Clash of the Decade?', CEPS, No. 285, 31 October, http://www.ceps.eu, pp. 4ff.

Romerstein, Herbert and Levchenko, Stanislav, *The KGB Against the 'Main Enemy'* (Lexington, MA: Lexington Books, 1989).

Romerstein, Herbert, *Soviet Active Measures and Propaganda: 'New Thinking' and Influence Activities in the Gorbachev Era* (Toronto: Mackenzie Institute for the Study of Terrorism, Revolution and Propaganda, 1989).

Russian Federation, Government of, 'Draft Program for the Effective Exploitation on A Systemic Basis of Foreign Policy Factors for the Purposes of the Long-term Development of the Russian Federation, as of 10 February 2010', MFA, excerpted in *Russian Newsweek*, 11 May 2010. (*Johnson's Russia List*, No. 96, 17 May 2010.)

Russian Federation, Government of, *Proekt Dogovora o evropeyskoy bezopasnosti* [Draft Treaty on European Security], 29 November 2009, http://kremlin.ru/news/6152.

Russian Federation, Government of, *Kontseptsiya Vneshney Politiki Rossiyskoy Federatsii* [*Foreign Policy Concepts of the Russian Federation*], December 1992.

Russian Federation, Government of, *Obzor Vneshney Politiki Rossiyskoy Federatsii* [*Foreign Policy Review of the Russian Federation*], 431, 27 March 2007, kremlin.ru.

Russian Federation, Government of, *Energeticheskaya strategiya Rossii na period do 2020* [*Energy Strategy of Russia to 2020*], 28 August 2003, No 1234-g.

Russian Federation, Law 'On the Bodies of the Federal Security Service', 12 April 1995.

Russian Federation, President, *The National Security Strategy of the Russian Federation to 2020*, 13 May 2009.

Schultz, Richard and Godson, Roy, *Dezinformatsia: Active Measures in Soviet Strategy* (Oxford: Pergamon-Brassey's, 1984).

Shelov-Kovedyayev, Fedor, *Strategiya i taktika vneshney politiki Rossii v novom zarubezh'ye* [*Strategy and Tactics of Russian Foreign Policy in the New Abroad*], MFA Report, September 1992.

Sherr, James, *Living with Russia in the Post-Soviet Era* (Camberley: Soviet Studies Research Centre, F31, July 1992).

Sherr, James, *The Mortgaging of Ukraine's Independence*, Chatham House Briefing Paper REP BP 2010/01, August 2010, pp. 6–10.

Sherr, James, *Russia and the West: A Reassessment*, The Shrivenham Papers, No. 6, Defence Academy of the United Kingdom, January 2008.

Sherr, James, 'Russia: Geopolitics and Crime', *The World Today*, Vol. 51, No. 2, February 1995.

Sherr, James, 'The Russia–EU Energy Relationship: Getting It Right', *The International Spectator*, Vol. 45, Rome.

Sherr, James and Main, Steven, *Russian and Ukrainian Perceptions of Events in Yugoslavia* (Camberley: Conflict Studies Research Centre, May 1999).

Shevtsova, Lilia, *Odinochkaya Derzhava: Pochemu Rossiya ne stala Zapadom i pochemu Rossii trudno s zapadom* [*Lonely Power: Why Russia Will Not Become Western and Why Russia Will Remain Difficult for the West*] (Moscow: Moscow Carnegie Centre, 2010).

Smith, Mark, *Russia and the Far Abroad: Aspects of Foreign Policy* (Camberley: Conflict Studies Research Centre, F39, May 1994).

Smith, Mark, *Russia and the Transformation of NATO*, UK Defence Academy, 11 January 2011.

Snyder, Jack, *The Soviet Strategic Culture: Implications for Limited Nuclear Operations* (Santa Monica, CA: Rand Corporation, 1977).

Socor, Vladimir, 'Implications of Ukraine's Gas Imports from Europe', *Eurasia Daily Monitor*, Vol. 10, Issue 60, 1 April 2013.

Stone, Norman, *World War One: A Short History* (London: Penguin, 2008).

Strang, Lord, 'The Moscow Negotiations, 1939', in Dilks, David (ed.), *Retreat from Power: Studies in Britain's Foreign Policy of the Twentieth Century, Vol. I 1906–1939* (London: Macmillan, 1981).

Sutela, Pekka, 'How Strong is Russia's Economic Foundation?', Policy Brief, Centre for European Reform, London, October 2009.

Thom, Françoise, *Les Fins du Communisme* (Paris: Criterion, 1994).

Thom, Françoise, 'La politique étrangère de la Russie' ['Russia's Foreign Policy'], *Commentaire*, No. 139, Autumn 2012.

Trenin, Dmitri, *Post-Imperium* (Washington, DC: Carnegie Endowment, 2011).

Tretyakov, Sergey and Earley, Pete, *Comrade J: The Untold Secrets of Russia's Master Spy in America After the End of the Cold War* (New York, Berkley Books, 2007).

Troitsky, Mikhail, 'Containment Must be Overcome', *Russia in Global Affairs Online*, 25 December 2010.

Tschepurin, Alexander, 'Orientir: kongress sootehestvennikov' ['Guide to the Congress of Compatriots'], *Mezhdunarodnaya Zhizn'* [*International Affairs*], No. 6, 2009.

Tsygankov, Andrey, *What is China to Us? Westernizers and Sinophiles in Russian Foreign Policy*, *Russie.Nei.Visions*, No. 45 (Paris: IFRI, December 2009).

Valdai Club, RIA-Novosti and Council on Foreign and Defence Policy, *Russia Should Not Miss Its Chance* (Moscow: Valdai Discussion Club Analytical Report, November 2011).

Vatansever, Adnan, *Russia's Oil Exports: Economic Rationale Versus Strategic Gains* (Carnegie Papers, No. 116, December 2010).

Vigor, Peter, *The Soviet View of War, Peace and Neutrality* (London: Routledge & Kegan Paul, 1975).

de Waal, Thomas, 'Spring for the Patriarchs', *The National Interest*, 27 January 2011.

Wojcik, Teresa, 'German Environmentalists Paid by Gazprom', 13 April 2011; 'Gazprom Lobbyists in Europe', 5 June 2011, and 'Russian Assault on Shale', 8 December 2011, Freepl.info.

Wood, Andrew, *Russia's Business Diplomacy*, Chatham House Briefing Paper, REP RSP BP 2011/02, May 2011.

Yeltsin, Boris, Interview with *Argumentiy i Faktiy*, No. 42, October 1992.

Yeltsin, Boris, Speech to the Federal Counter-Intelligence Service (FSK), 26 May 1994.

Yurgens, Igor et al., *Russia in the Twenty-first Century: Vision for the Future* (Moscow, Institute for Contemporary Development), January 2010.

The Russia and Eurasia Programme

The Russia and Eurasia Programme at Chatham House brings together the best thinking on the changing dynamics of the countries of the former Soviet Union as well as their implications for the West and the wider world. The Programme comprises both in-house staff and an international network of associate fellows, all leading area specialists, who together provide maximum geographical and thematic coverage of the region.

For more information visit:
www.chathamhouse.org/research/russia-eurasia